BFI Film Classics

The BFI Film Classics series introduces, interprets and celebrates landmarks of world cinema. Each volume offers an argument for the film's 'classic' status, together with discussion of its production and reception history, its place within a genre or national cinema, an account of its technical and aesthetic importance, and in many cases, the author's personal response to the film.

For a full list of titles in the series, please visit
https://www.bloomsbury.com/uk/series/bfi-film-classics/

MW00469242

In memory of David Geoffrey Weir

'Finché c'è morte c'è speranza.'

Giuseppe Tomasi di Lampedusa

The Leopard
[Il gattopardo]

David Weir

THE BRITISH FILM INSTITUTE
Bloomsbury Publishing Plc
50 Bedford Square, London, WC1B 3DP, UK
1385 Broadway, New York, NY 10018, USA
29 Earlsfort Terrace, Dublin 2, Ireland

BLOOMSBURY is a trademark of Bloomsbury Publishing Plc

First published in Great Britain 2024 by Bloomsbury on behalf of the
British Film Institute
21 Stephen Street, London W1T 1LN
www.bfi.org.uk

The BFI is the lead organisation for film in the UK and the distributor of Lottery funds for film.
Our mission is to ensure that film is central to our cultural life, in particular by supporting and
nurturing the next generation of filmmakers and audiences. We serve a public role which covers
the cultural, creative and economic aspects of film in the UK.

Cover artwork: © Simone Riccardi
Series cover design: Louise Dugdale
Series text design: Ketchup/SE14
Images from *The Leopard* (Luchino Visconti, 1963), Titanus/La Société Nouvelle Pathé-
Cinéma/Société Générale Cinématographique; *Golden Parable* (Vittorio De Seta, 1955), Astra
Cinematografica; *Teresa Venerdi* (Vittorio De Sica, 1941), Alleanza Cinematografica Italiana/Europa
Film; *The Earth Trembles* (Luchino Visconti, 1948), Universalia; *The Godfather* (Francis Ford Coppola,
1972), © Paramount Pictures Corporation; *The Age of Innocence* (Martin Scorsese, 1993), © Columbia
Pictures Industries, Inc.
Film stills courtesy BFI National Archive

A catalogue record for this book is available from the British Library.

A catalog record for this book is available from the Library of Congress.

ISBN: PB: 978-1-8390-2615-7
          ePDF: 978-1-8390-2617-1
          ePUB: 978-1-8390-2616-4

Produced for Bloomsbury Publishing Plc by Sophie Contento
Printed and bound in India

To find out more about our authors and books visit www.bloomsbury.com
and sign up for our newsletters.

Contents

Acknowledgments

The number of academic, editorial and other *aristoi* who have played an outsize role in the making of this little book could fill the ballroom of the Palazzo Gangi, or, at least, one of those golden salons just off the dancefloor. Allow me to bow in appreciation to Isabella Bertoletti of the Fashion Institute of Technology and Alejandro Cuadrado of Columbia University, for translation; in respect to Bénédicte Coste of the Université de Bourgogne, Rossana Capitano of the University of Warwick, David Forgacs of New York University and Rosa Di Maria of the Villa Boscogrande, for information; in gratitude to Giovanna Bosman and Cristiana Pipitone of the Fondazione Gramsci in Rome, John Calhoun of the Billy Rose Theatre Division at the New York Public Library, Michael Gundert of the Cooper Union Library in New York and Genevieve Maxwell of the Margaret Herrick Library in Beverly Hills, for investigation; in acknowledgment to Valeria de Chirico of Cappelli Editore in Bologna, Eugenio Semboloni of the Biblioteca di storia moderna e contemporanea in Rome and Nicoletta Lanza Tomasi in Palermo, for permission (to publish, respectively, the two production photos of set construction for *The Leopard*; the etching of Camillo Benso, Count of Cavour; and the portrait of Prince Giulio Fabrizio Tomasi); in reverence to the three anonymous readers of the manuscript, for direction (and correction); and in admiration to Jane Desmarais, J. Hoberman and Imogen Sara Smith, for inspiration. *Mille grazie a tutti*!

Please permit a deeper bow to those nobles who have worked so hard to make my efforts seem more polished than ever I might have hoped: *molte, molte grazie* to Simone Riccardi for cover art; to Louise Dugdale for cover design; and to Phillipa Hudson for editing. I also request the humble honour of kissing the hand of those three gentle but efficient ladies who grace that elegant Palazzo of Publication in the London Borough of Camden: the Marchesa di Piazza Bedford, Veidehi Hans, for her faultless administration; the Duchessa di Freelancia, Sophie Contento, for her matchless management of production; and the Principessa di Bloomsbury herself, Rebecca Barden, for her peerless perfectionism, all the more impressive for being touched so completely with kindness and generosity.

E infine, ma non da ultimo, alla mia compagna di vita, Camille: molto più che grazie, molto di più – il mio amore, il mio cuore.

The Italian peninsula before unification

1 The Source

'If we want things to stay as they are, things will have to change':[1]
so says the young Duke Tancredi Falconeri (Alain Delon), beloved
nephew of Prince Fabrizio (Burt Lancaster), a Sicilian nobleman
for whom any real change to his aristocratic world can only
mean decline. The remark is made early on in Luchino Visconti's
Il gattopardo (*The Leopard*, 1963) when Tancredi announces his
plans to join the red-shirted rebels of General Garibaldi's army to
help liberate the Kingdom of the Two Sicilies from Spanish Bourbon
rule and unify the disparate imperial provinces, aristocratic duchies
and ecclesiastical states of the Italian peninsula into a modern
nation. The line is easily the most famous one in the film, as it is in
the 1958 novel by Giuseppe Tomasi di Lampedusa on which the
film is based and from which it is quoted verbatim: 'Se vogliamo
che tutto rimanga com'è, bisogna che tutto cambi.'[2] Both the novel
and the film make clear that Tancredi is no republican nationalist
in fact; rather, he is a reactionary opportunist intent on using the
nineteenth-century revolution known as the Risorgimento (the word
means resurgence, as in 'resurgence of nationalism') to preserve
the privileges of his class. Indeed, the famous line about the need
for change to preserve the status quo is preceded by Tancredi's
explanation for 'revolutionary' action: 'Unless we ourselves take a
hand now, they'll foist a republic on us' (p. 28). This tension between
reaction and revolution, between sameness and change, manifests
itself in both the novel and the film in multiple ways and in different
guises: tradition vies with transformation; aristocratic custom with
bourgeois convention; high culture with low politics; decadence with
progress. That last pairing is the most profound one of all, since it
encompasses all the others: decadence as Visconti understood it is
removed from such popular conceptions as hedonistic excess and

perverse dissipation; rather, it is the artistic interpretation of social change as cultural decline, the kind of decadence exemplified by those great European writers the director most admired: Gabriele D'Annunzio, Marcel Proust, Thomas Mann and, indeed, Giuseppe Tomasi di Lampedusa.[3]

In *The Leopard* (both book and film), all the political and aesthetic tensions are mapped onto a larger conflict that is perhaps the most profound one in modern Italian history: the problem of inequality that emerged with the Risorgimento between the wealthy, industrial North of Italy and the impoverished, agricultural South – what the Italian Marxist philosopher Antonio Gramsci called 'the Southern Question'.[4] Gramsci had argued that the people of the South did not enjoy the alleged benefits of Italian unification because the Risorgimento was a 'passive revolution' – '"revolution" without "a revolution"' in that 'unity had not taken place on a basis of equality, but as hegemony of the North over the Mezzogiorno' (literally, 'midday' or 'noon', a metonym for 'the South') whereby the North 'enriched itself at the expense of the South'.[5] In Gramsci's view, the Risorgimento had not reformed society but simply transformed it without addressing underlying social issues – a political condition that Gramsci termed *trasformismo* (transformism).[6]

Gramsci's transformist observations date from the early 1920s but had long been recognised as a problem endemic to the Risorgimento. As the Tuscan politician Sidney Sonnino wrote in 1877, '[I]n Sicily our institutions are based on a merely formal liberalism and have just given the oppressing class a legal means of continuing as they always have.'[7] This formulation is very like Tancredi's cynical remark that the only way to maintain aristocratic privilege is by supporting the nationalist revolution to ensure profitable participation in the new government. Of course, this craven, almost Machiavellian decadence is presented in the novel as a necessity, a new fact of life, without the kind of moral judgement that animated Gramsci and scores of mid-century Italian Marxists – like Visconti. In the novel, such judgement is replaced by resignation to the odious political realities of the Risorgimento on the part of the Prince and by bemused irony on the part of Lampedusa.

Giuseppe Tomasi, Principe di Lampedusa, Duca di Palma di Montechiaro (1896–1957) was a Sicilian nobleman whose family history is thinly fictionalised in the novel published a year after his death. The title *Il gattopardo* derives from the animal on the Lampedusa family crest, which despite the translated title *The Leopard* is not a leopard in fact but a serval, a much smaller spotted feline. Prince Fabrizio Salina, the eponymous *gattopardo* of the novel, is based on Lampedusa's paternal great-great-grandfather, Giulio Fabrizio Ferdinando Francesco Baldassare Melchiorre Salvatore Antonino Domenico Rosario Gaetano Tomasi, VIII Principe di Lampedusa, IX Duca di Palma (1813–85). How much the historical Tomasi and the fictional Salina have in common is hard to say, aside from superficial resemblances such as their shared love of astronomy, a character trait which Visconti registers in the *mise en scène* of the film (the telescopes and astrolabes we see are those originally owned by the historical prince).[8]

Giulio Fabrizio Ferdinando Francesco Baldassare Melchiorre Salvatore Antonino Domenico Rosario Gaetano Tomasi, VIII Principe di Lampedusa, IX Duca di Palma (painter unknown, oil on canvas, mid-nineteenth century) (courtesy Nicoletta Lanza Tomasi, Duchessa di Palma)

The melancholy resignation to the decline of the aristocracy in the face of political and social change may well be a psychological projection onto his ancestor by Lampedusa. But whatever the source it is crucial to the character of the Prince, whose melancholy awareness of

The Prince in his observatory

his own social and political demise infuses the tone of the writing throughout, as in this key sentence early on: 'Between the pride and intellectuality of his mother and the sensuality and irresponsibility of his father, poor Prince Fabrizio lived in perpetual discontent ..., watching the ruin of his own class and his own inheritance without ever making, still less wanting to make, any move toward saving it' (p. 9). Such elegant resignation to the declining fortunes of the Italian aristocracy no doubt resonated with Visconti, given the decline of his own noble clan over his lifetime.[9]

Salina knows that his profligate brother-in-law has exhausted the patrimony of his nephew Tancredi (the name derives from the Christian knight Tancredi, the crusading hero of Torquato Tasso's epic poem, *La Gerusalemme liberata*, 1581), so he feels an obligation to his dead sister to support her son. Even though such support will only further 'the ruin of his own class', Salina no less than his nephew can read the signs of the times. The Prince understands that Tancredi's only recourse is to marry money:

Tancredi, he considered, had a great future; he would be the standard-bearer of a counterattack which the nobility, under new trappings, could launch against the new social State. To do this he lacked only one thing: money; this Tancredi did not have; none at all. And to get on in politics, now that a name counted less, would require a lot of money: money to buy votes, money to do the electors favors, money for a dazzling style of living. (pp. 70–1)

He will also require a wife 'capable of helping an ambitious and brilliant husband to climb the slippery slopes of the new society' (p. 71). The cynical acknowledgment here that Tancredi's social success depends on a combination of political corruption and cultural refinement could not be more decadent. That decadence is compounded by the aristocratic misogyny that recognises how important a clever, attractive woman is to the rear-guard political manoeuvring the Prince contemplates. His own daughter Concetta is in love with his nephew, but he knows that her dowry will not be adequate to Tancredi's future needs. Still, 'They'd make a fine couple,' the Prince muses to himself. 'But I fear Tancredi will have to aim higher, by which of course I mean lower' (p. 42).

The perfect opportunity for Tancredi to resolve his financial problems comes when he accompanies his uncle to the village of Donnafugata in southern Sicily, where Don Fabrizio has an estate that still preserves the feudal traditions of old. Increasingly aware of the importance of reconciling himself to the new political reality so 'things can stay as they are', the Prince invites the nouveau-riche bourgeois landowner and mayor of Donnafugata, Don Calogero Sedàra, to dine at his palace. The mayor arrives with his beautiful, lively daughter Angelica: Tancredi is smitten, Concetta is crushed and Salina relieved that his nephew has found a woman who – unlike his own daughter – could be 'ambassadress in Vienna, or Petersburg' (p. 71), thanks to a finishing school in Florence. The narrative continues with Tancredi's romance of Angelica, paralleled by Salina's 'romance' of Angelica's father, that is, his financial negotiations with Don Calogero over the daughter's dowry. Tancredi, meanwhile, continues to advance his military career by moving down in rank from captain to lieutenant, a paradox explained by shifting his allegiance from the 'rabble' of red-shirted Garibaldini to the 'real army', that of 'His Majesty, King of Sardinia' (p. 149).

This would be Vittorio Emanuele II, soon to assume the title King of Italy, confirming Tancredi's cynical instinct for picking winners.

The Prince, by contrast, declines the invitation to align his own interests with those of the new nationalist regime. The Cavaliere Aimone Chevalley di Monterzuolo, an emissary from Vittorio Emanuele's recently formed government, journeys to Donnafugata to ask Salina to represent Sicily as senator. The Prince declines the honour, explaining at great length the reasons for his refusal, his response forming one of the most poetic stretches of the novel that is also one of the most ideological. The Sicilian explains to the Piedmontese that he belongs 'to an unfortunate generation, swung between the old world and the new, ... ill at ease in both'. Moreover, he is 'without illusions', and so 'lacks the faculty of self-deception, essential requisite for wanting to guide others' (p. 180). Besides, Sicily is irredeemable, a land of 'voluptuous immobility', its people so 'worn out and exhausted' their only desire is oblivion (pp. 177–8). At the end of the interview, the Prince tells Chevalley that he should seek for senators among the younger generation to find men 'who are good at masking, at blending, I should say, their personal interests with vague public ideals'. This sounds as though Salina is on the point of recommending his nephew Tancredi, but no: the man Chevalley wants, he says, is Sedàra, who has something better than prestige – 'he has power' (p. 181).

In a letter to a friend, Lampedusa explains that his story evoking 'a Sicilian nobleman at a moment of crisis (not to be taken to mean simply that of 1860), how he reacts to it and how the degeneration of the family becomes ever more marked until it reaches almost total collapse' is 'seen from within, with a certain connivance of the author' (pp. xi–xii). That 'connivance' includes many allusions to events in the future that are, of course, outside the consciousness of the characters but predicted by the history they experience. Some of these anachronisms are merely clever, as when, after she accepts the marriage proposal, Angelica plants a kiss on Salina's cheek and whispers, 'Uncle mine!' – Tancredi's own favoured form of endearment. The narrator finds the line 'highly successful …, comparable in its perfect timing almost to Eisenstein's baby carriage' (p. 138), a reference to the Odessa Steps sequence in *Bronenosets Potemkin* (*Battleship Potemkin*, 1925).

Other anachronisms offer insight into later developments outside the timeframe of the present narrative that insert Lampedusa's fiction into Italian history. For example, after Salina recommends Sedàra to Chevalley as a candidate for the new Italian Senate, Chevalley is startled at the suggestion because he has been following the mayor's career and knows how unscrupulous the man is, but he holds his tongue, whereupon the narrator adds: 'and he did well not to compromise himself, as ten years later Don Calogero did in fact gain the Senate' (p. 181). But by far the most interesting of these anachronisms comes when the Prince reflects on the stunted life of Don Ciccio Tumeo, his shooting companion at Donnafugata, and is 'touched by the dignity of his poverty'. The reflection occasions this remarkable commentary: 'Don Fabrizio could not know it then, but a great deal of the slackness and acquiescence for which the people of the South were to be criticized during the next decades was due to the stupid annulment of the first expression of liberty ever offered them' (p. 113). This kind of omniscience might have been conveyed in Visconti's film by means of voiceover narration, but the director chose not to employ that device (although some early screenplay drafts include it) because he did not have to: the Italian audience for the film in 1963 would have been acutely aware of the persistence of Gramsci's 'Southern Question' during their own miraculous economic times.

The ideology of Lampedusa's novel is easy to criticise as retrograde if the focus remains on Salina – as in his long philosophical explanation to Chevalley on the irredeemable character of the Sicilian people – but there is sufficient commentary about political history (like the one concerning the annulment of liberty in the Mezzogiorno) to suggest that Visconti might well have been drawn to the novel for its relevance to contemporary ideological concerns.

After *The Leopard* was published and became a massive bestseller, the critical reception was so fraught that it soon came to be known as *il caso Lampedusa* (the Lampedusa case). Opinion was divided over whether such a traditional novel could be anything other than reactionary, the assumption being that avant-garde technique necessarily aligns with progressive ideology. The publisher Elio Vittorini tried to justify his rejection of the manuscript that Giangiacomo Feltrinelli had published by claiming that it was 'right-wing', a view seconded by the Communist Party press.[10] Leaving aside the fact that Feltrinelli had been a member of the PCI (Partito Comunista Italiano/Italian Communist Party), fighting against the Nazis and Fascists in World War II, Marxist arguments against Lampedusa as a reactionary author were undercut when Louis Aragon, one of the foremost leftists of the post-war period, read *The Leopard* after it was translated into French in 1959 and pronounced it 'one of the great novels of all time'. Aragon added that the novel offered an unrelenting critique of the Sicilian aristocracy that made it, yes, 'left-wing'.[11] The Lampedusa 'case' was not exactly settled when the producer Goffredo Lombardo asked Visconti to adapt the novel to the screen, so it makes sense to understand the film, at least in part, as the director's entry into an active ideological debate.

Literature and cinema each have their separate superiorities over the other, and some of the changes that Visconti made to the story reflect basic differences in the representational strengths of the two media. In the novel, for example, Lampedusa merely alludes to Garibaldi's landing at Marsala and his ensuing victory at Palermo, whereas Visconti takes full advantage of the opportunity for spectacle that cinema affords by staging the battle in full over some eight minutes of the film. He omits three chapters from the novel: two because they would have distracted from the historical narrative and one because it would have been all but unfilmable. The first chapter outside the diegesis of the film is 'Father Pirrone Pays a Visit', in which the Jesuit priest-in-residence with the Salina family travels to his home village and resolves the problems posed by his pregnant niece (the episode serves as a comic, peasant counterpart to the aristocratic arrangements Salina makes to facilitate the union of Angelica and Tancredi). The second chapter Visconti omits for diegetic reasons is 'Relics' (set in May 1910), the conclusion of the novel that details the stunted lives of Concetta and her sisters, all superannuated spinsters who venerate a collection of holy relics that turn out to be fake. The 'unfilmable' chapter is 'Death of the Prince' (set in July 1888), wherein the third-person limited form of the narration intensifies, with Lampedusa presenting Salina's last moments from the highly poetic and deeply moving perspective of the dying man. Elsewhere, Visconti externalises the Prince's internal commentary on events as dialogue (sometimes spoken by the Prince himself, sometimes by other characters), but it is hard to see how that strategy could have been used for the death scene. Instead, Visconti concludes *The Leopard* with another interpolation that balances against the interpolated battle scene early on: that extended spectacle showing Garibaldi's red-shirted republicans at war is countered by the sounds of some of those same soldiers, now adjudged to be rebels disloyal to the new monarchy, being executed by firing squad. The action occurs after Colonel Pallavicino (the only historical figure to appear in both novel and film) recounts to Salina at the banquet following the great ball how he carried out his orders to stop the advance of Garibaldi by firing on him and his men at the Battle of Aspromonte, wounding the general and taking him prisoner. By adding the sounds of the execution to the historical material in Lampedusa's fiction, Visconti effectively suggests how entangled sameness and change, reaction and revolution, had become during the Risorgimento and, by implication, during the director's own times.

Lampedusa's posthumous novel was published in 1958 and Visconti's film was released in 1963: those dates bracket the period of post-war prosperity in Italy known as *il miracolo economico*. But Italy's 'economic miracle' was mostly confined to the North, with the people of the South largely excluded from the opportunities that allowed their countrymen in Lombardia, Piedmonte and other

A scene from Vittorio De Seta's *Golden Parable* (1955)

northern provinces to elevate their standard of living and enter the middle class. A series of remarkable documentaries by Vittorio De Seta made in the mid-1950s offer a valuable visual record of just how impoverished the people of the South remained as those of other regions began to reap the benefits of an industrialised economy. Filming in colour using the widescreen format CinemaScope and stereophonic sound, De Seta shows in a series of ten short films (most about ten minutes, the longest around twenty) how farmers, fishermen, shepherds and miners go about their everyday lives in Sardinia, Sicily and Calabria. In *Parabola d'oro* (*Golden Parable*, 1955), for example, we see Sicilian wheat farmers harvesting the golden grain, transporting it by mule, then threshing it by hand. Unusually for Italian cinema, De Seta used direct sound, but without narration: we hear wind rustling the wheat, insects chirping, the whisk of sickles cutting stalks of grain and a distant peasant singing. When these films were rediscovered, restored and screened in 2005, many viewers saw the pre-industrial world of southern Italy represented in them not as harsh reality or proof of political inequality but as visual poetry of great beauty, almost mythic in its evocative emotional power.

The relevance of De Seta's documentaries for Visconti's *The Leopard* lies in the visual evidence they offer for Tancredi's cynical opportunism: things may have changed when the Italian peninsula became the Italian nation, but they remained the same for the people of the South. Indeed, the ancestors of those farmers and fishermen in De Seta's films must have been as unaffected by the Risorgimento in the 1860s as their descendants were by the economic miracle of the 1950s and 60s. If contemporary audiences for De Seta's documentaries find their political vision clouded by the beauty of the films, the same is true of Visconti's *The Leopard*. The tension between politics and art is a constant in Visconti's career, but that tension is compounded in *The Leopard* because his treatment of the historical subject of the Risorgimento occurred in the contemporary context of *il miracolo economico*. How much Visconti meant for his lush evocation of the past to be a political commentary on the present remains an open question. But some of Visconti's more radical contemporaries seized on the cinematic imbalance – if that's what it is – between the sumptuous, saturated *mise en scène* of *The Leopard* and the critique implicit in the scenario about self-interested aristocrats manoeuvring to take advantage of nationalist sentiments for social and financial benefit and accused the director of being no different from the detached aristocratic aesthete whose work he had adapted for the screen. The criticism goes to the heart of Visconti's paradoxical identity as an aristocratic Communist (or would that be a Communist aristocrat?) whose social critique of decadence was bound up with his aesthetic veneration for it.

2 The Director

The charge against Visconti for being 'decadent' is understandable given the director's aristocratic background and artistic interests – interests that became more apparent as his career developed. Indeed, towards the end of his life, Visconti described himself on more than one occasion as 'un décadente'. In 1976, he claimed to be 'very pleased' to have the epithet applied to him because it made him part of the great tradition of European decadence that included 'Rimbaud, Verlaine, Baudelaire, Huysmans. But above all Marcel Proust and Thomas Mann.'[12] In 1975, he admitted to having 'a very high opinion of "decadence"' (the scare quotes signalling distance from popular misconceptions of decadence as mere immorality or perversity), adding, 'I am imbued with its spirit.' Once again, he evoked Mann to place himself in a continuing cultural tradition: 'Mann was a decadent of German culture, I of Italian formation. What has always interested me is the analysis of a sick society.'[13] While those comments were made with reference to *Gruppo di famiglia in un interno* (*Conversation Piece*, 1974), the reference to 'Italian formation' makes them relevant to *The Leopard*, which is nothing if not a cinematic analysis of 'a sick society'.

In 1985, Guido Aristarco, the founding editor of the influential film journal *Cinema nuovo*, took stock of Visconti's career and, revising an earlier, harsher assessment made when *The Leopard* was released (see Chapter 5), asked whether the director had been a 'critic or poet of decadence'. If decadence was Visconti's preferred mode of cinematic expression, did that aesthetic include an argument *against* decadence? Aristarco concluded that the films describe decadence but do not celebrate it: social critique trumps aesthetic indulgence.[14] Visconti's own comments, however, suggest a more ambivalent relation to the culture of decadence. Moreover, for Visconti decadence was not simply an intellectual or artistic problem – it was something personal. As a titled member of Italian nobility, he had a complex relationship to the spirit of decadence that 'imbued' his spirit – and not just because his homosexuality, in the eyes of Catholic conservatives, would mark him off as 'decadent' by definition. As a member of a centuries-old line of northern Italian aristocrats, he had first-hand knowledge of the threat that bourgeois modernity posed to the privileges of class and culture the old order entailed. At the same time, as a member of the Italian Communist Party, he aligned himself with the progressive political forces that countered the (declining) aristocratic society into which he had been born. Archibald Colquhoun, who translated Lampedusa's novel into English and worked as dialogue coach on the film, captured the contradictions in the director's sensibility when he observed that Visconti 'thinks Left and lives Right'.[15]

In *The Leopard*, both the would-be liberal order of the new Italy and the retrograde politics of the decadent aristocracy of the old seem compromised, with each affected – possibly infected – by the other. These two dimensions of the film are interrelated and entangled, and it takes no great effort to see the dual concerns of *The Leopard* as reflective of a like duality in the director's sensibility produced by the conflict of his old-world upbringing and the tumultuous politics of modern Italy. After an initial infatuation with Fascism in the early 1930s, Visconti experienced a political volte-face later in the decade and came very close to being executed in 1944 for his involvement in the Italian resistance. This intense period is memorialised in the powerful documentary *Giorni di gloria* (*Days of Glory*, 1945), for which Visconti shot several scenes, including the trial and execution, by firing squad, of Pietro Koch, the anti-partisan leader who ran the prison where Visconti had been held and beaten. After the war, Visconti appeared on track to commit himself to social progress and produce the type of cinematic art reflective of such commitment. That direction is manifest in his second feature, *La terra trema* (*The Earth Trembles*, 1948), a classic of neorealism about Sicilian fishermen which was financed by the Italian Communist Party. But somewhere along the way Visconti's penchant for decadence asserted itself, and he closed out his career by making a series of films imbued with its spirit, ending with *L'innocente* (*The Innocent*, 1976), a Technicolor melodrama about *fin-de-siècle* aristocrats based on a novel by Gabriele D'Annunzio, the one author most responsible for the literary movement known as *decadentismo*. Visconti's passage from *neorealismo* to *decadentismo* does suggest the transit from political commitment to artistic excess, but the polarities implied by such terms are misleading. Perhaps it is safer to say, simply, that Visconti remained sympathetic to conflicting social systems and aesthetic values, his art somehow accommodating the tensions such conflict entails.

Visconti was born in 1906 to a wealthy Milanese family whose aristocratic roots went back centuries, as evidenced by a reference to one Ugolino Visconti in the eighth canto of Dante's *Purgatorio*.[16] Another ancestor appears in Geoffrey Chaucer's *The Canterbury Tales*, where we read of one 'Barnabo de Lumbardia': 'Of Melan grete barnabo Viscounte, / God of delit and scourge of lumbardye.'[17] During his Italian campaign, Napoléon Bonaparte conferred the dukedom of Modrone on Visconti's ancestors when the family afforded the French cavalry grazing rights to their land in the north (Visconti's father, Giuseppe, laid claim to the title Duca di Modrone, while Luchino became known as the Conte di Modrone). Visconti's mother, Carla Erba, was the daughter of a bourgeois family that made its fortune in pharmaceuticals.[18] (This biographical detail is echoed in *The Leopard* when the aristocratic Tancredi, whose ancestors have exhausted the family fortune, marries the daughter of the wealthy bourgeois mayor, Don Calogero Sedàra.) As was the custom among aristocratic families in belle époque Milan, the Viscontis supported La Scala, the famed opera house, after it lost state funding. Visconti's love of opera (which dates from his childhood) cannot be overstated: by the end of his career, he had directed more operas (seventeen) than feature films (fourteen).[19] Indeed, the love of opera helps to account for the two most 'operatic' elements in many Visconti films: the ornate *mise en scène* and the melodramatic plotting.

The latter quality is evident in his very first film, *Ossessione* (*Obsession*, 1943), about a vagrant who finds work at a petrol station in the Po Valley near Ferrara, seduces the owner's wife, and then conspires with her to murder the husband, making his death look like a traffic accident. The man's passions cool when he suspects – along with the police – that the woman has used him to cash in on her husband's life insurance. The couple reconcile and are on the point of getting away with murder when the woman is killed in another traffic accident. The sensational scenario is based on *The Postman Always Rings Twice* (1934), the pulp crime novel by James M. Cain first adapted by Pierre Chenal as *Le dernier tournant* (The last turning) (1939) and later by Tay Garnett in 1946. Visconti became interested in Cain's bestseller thanks to Jean Renoir, who gave him a French translation of the novel when he was working as the uncredited third assistant director (in charge of costumes) on *Partie de campagne* (*A Day in the Country*, 1946). Visconti's disenchantment with Italian Fascism drew him to France during the period of the Popular Front, the antifascist coalition of Socialists and Communists that controlled the government from 1936 to 1938. Renoir was Visconti's elder by only twelve years, but he seems to have been something of a father figure to the young aristocrat struggling to find his place in the world (for a while, Visconti made a name for himself breeding champion racehorses). Some sources claim, erroneously, that Visconti assisted on Renoir's earlier *Toni* (1935),[20] a film about immigrant workers in southern France. The confusion is instructive: *Toni* is now regarded as a neorealist film *avant la lettre* because of the combination of working-class subject matter, non-professional actors (speaking a range of provincial dialects) and location shooting.

When Visconti made *Obsession*, he was not as actively antifascist as he would later become, but the visual style of the film departs so radically from the art deco Hollywood aesthetic of the 'white telephone' (*telefoni bianchi*) films of the era that an implicit political

A 'white telephone'
film: Vittorio De Sica's
Teresa Venerdì (1941)

statement is made thereby. *Telefoni bianchi* were escapist comedies
made at the Cinecittà Studios (founded by Mussolini in 1937) and
directed by some of the same people who would go on to become
better known today as neorealists, such as Vittorio De Sica. Despite
the absence of overt ideological content, *Obsession* is understood
today as the first example of Italian neorealism, in part because Mario
Serandrei, Visconti's editor, coined the term *neorealismo* when he
viewed the rushes of the film.[21] But *Obsession* can hardly be called
'pure' neorealism because the film did not – and could not – reflect
the wartime and post-war realities of Italian life. Of course, 'pure
neorealism' is a phantom category since scant agreement exists on
what constitutes neorealism in the first place. That said, Roberto
Rossellini's and De Sica's realist treatments of Nazi occupation and
post-war economic distress in, respectively, *Roma città aperta* (*Rome,
Open City*, 1945) and *Ladri di biciclette* (*Bicycle Thieves*, 1948) struck
a chord with contemporary audiences who had first-hand knowledge
of those very experiences. As a result, neorealism became less of a
style, genre or movement (though it is all those as well) and more of an
ethos. The novelist Italo Calvino called neorealism 'the general climate
of the time, … a moral tension that was in the air … not so much an
artistic phenomenon, more a physical, existential, collective need'.[22]

The Earth Trembles
(1948): visual poetry vs
Communist polemic

Calvino's comments concern literary neorealism, but they
seem especially relevant in support of the neorealist credentials
of Visconti's second film, *The Earth Trembles*, although, strictly
speaking, the recent war does not play a noticeable role in his free
adaptation of Giovanni Verga's 1881 novel about the disintegration
of a family of Sicilian fishermen (*I Malavoglia*, the Italian title of the
novel, literally means 'the reluctant ones' and refers to a family of
fishermen called Toscano, which Visconti renames Valastro). Visconti
departed from the usual neorealist practice of post-synchronisation
by using direct sound, as Renoir had done in *Toni*, and achieved a
powerful sense of realism, not only by means of location shooting
in the village of Aci Trezza near Catania, but also by having non-
professional actors improvise scenes in local dialect.[23] In the novel,
the decline of the family results primarily from natural causes,
whereas the film puts the emphasis on social forces, as the prologue
makes clear: 'The story which the film tells is the same all over the
world and is repeated every year everywhere that people exploit
other people.' The agents of exploitation are a group of mafia-
like wholesalers who take advantage of the poor fishermen, never
offering a fair price for their daily catch. 'Ntoni, the eldest son of the
Valastro family, tries to counter the wholesalers' grip on the market
by mortgaging the family home and going into business for himself.

But when his boat is destroyed in a storm, he cannot repay the debt and the bank evicts the family from their home. 'Ntoni is forced to work again for the men he despises, but he maintains his dignity in a moving speech to a young girl in which he explains that, while he may have failed to break free from an unjust system, the only hope for the future lies in collective action. That Communist message is less polemical on the screen than on the page, in part because it is delivered in Sicilian dialect by a real fisherman. But it is also true that the Communist content is muted by Visconti's visual poetry, an early example of the characteristic tension in his films between politics and aesthetics.

Criticism of Visconti's skilled exploitation of cinematic art as something that defused the political force of *The Earth Trembles* may have played a role in his third film, *Bellissima* (1951), which foregrounds the illusory, deceptive nature of cinema itself. The scenario concerns a working-class mother's fantasy that her young daughter can become a movie star when she enters the girl in a Cinecittà contest to find *la più bella bambina di Roma* (the most beautiful little girl in Rome). Anna Magnani plays Maddalena, the film-struck mother who almost bankrupts the family by paying acting coaches, dancing masters and dressmakers to transform her rather plain daughter into a child star. Visconti made the film at a time when he had come to question neorealism, and *Bellissima* is replete with implicit criticism of the movement – this despite being based on a story by Cesare Zavattini, the principal theorist of neorealism and De Sica's main screenwriter. For example, the scenario casts doubt on the neorealist practice of using non-professional actors, both in the story of the little girl and in a scene featuring Liliana Mancini, whose character explains how her life was ruined after a director cast her off the street for a role in a film – the real-life experience of Mancini herself, who appeared in the neorealist *Sotto il sole di Roma* (Under the sun of Rome) (1948) but whose career in front of the camera foundered thereafter. Also, Visconti undermines playfully the neorealist practice of location shooting by having the principal location be Cinecittà itself, in the backstudio tradition of Hollywood movies like *Sunset Blvd.* (1950). Because of her star-making performance in *Rome, Open City*, no actor was identified more completely with neorealism than Magnani. But Visconti has her undercut that identity in *Bellissima* when Maddalena tells her daughter that she will never become a movie star if she speaks Romanesco, the Roman dialect that animates Magnani's torrential speech throughout the film (as it also did in *Rome, Open City*).

Bellissima is sometimes cited as an example of *neorealismo rosa* (pink neorealism), a comic variation on neorealism proper that continues the tradition of *telefoni bianchi*, albeit in a different social register. Visconti's removal from neorealism, pink or otherwise, is all but absolute in his next full-length feature, *Senso* (1954). In fact, some film historians see *Senso* as a hinge point in the history of Italian cinema. The film came close to putting an end to neorealism altogether by shifting the focus from post-war Italy and the problems of the working class to the earlier historical period of the Risorgimento dominated by aristocratic elites.[24] But however much *Senso* may depart from the contemporary focus of his prior films (including the segment on Anna Magnani that he directed in the anthology film *Siamo donne* (*We, the Women*, 1953)), what it has in common with most of them is Visconti's enduring interest in melodrama.[25]

The word *melodrama* combines the Greek root related to music – μελο- or *melo-* (as in 'melody') – with the verb δρᾶν or *dran*, meaning 'to do, act, or perform'. The combination of music and action made melodrama especially well suited to early cinema, with the action of silent film accompanied by orchestra or piano. The exaggerated pantomime performance style of most silents helped to link early film melodramas with sensational action, but that connection had been around for some time, thanks to Italian *melodramma*, a synonym for opera. Visconti's preference for melodrama no doubt has as its primary impetus his love of opera, but that interest also found support in the immense appeal the genre had for audiences in the 1950s, who turned out in droves to see Hollywood features like Douglas Sirk's *All That Heaven Allows* (1955). Visconti's brand of melodrama differs from Sirk's and that of other Hollywood directors, such as Vincente Minnelli, mainly in the *mise en scène*, which in Sirk's cinematic world is artificial in the extreme, in contrast to Visconti's trademark authenticity. But Visconti opts for an operatic level of artificiality in the action, which in *Senso* is as emotionally overwrought as in any Sirk offering.

The 'Risorgimento melodrama' (a common epithet) of *Senso* concerns the Countess Livia Serpieri (Alida Valli), who supports the revolutionary actions of her cousin, Marchese Roberto Ussoni (Massimo Girotti) – not a member of the Italian army but the leader of a group of patriotic resistance fighters. Ussoni is forced into exile after he challenges the Austrian officer Franz Mahler (Farley Granger) to a duel, whereupon Livia tries to intercede on her cousin's behalf but instead falls in love with Mahler. The nadir of her betrayal comes when she gives Mahler the funds that the patriots have entrusted to her for safekeeping, which he uses to bribe a doctor to declare him unfit for military service. No less craven than the Austrian officer is Livia's husband Count Serpieri (Heinz Moog), whose political allegiances are driven purely by self-interest, as he negotiates with Italian patriots and Austrian occupiers alike to ensure that his fortune remains intact whatever the outcome of the conflict. In the end, Livia leaves her husband at his estate in Aldeno to be with her lover in Verona. Once there, she finds Mahler drunk, with a prostitute, and realises that the man has merely used her as a means to his unscrupulous ends. He mocks her relentlessly for her gullibility, whereupon she reports him as a deserter to his commanding officer. The final scene shows Mahler's execution by firing squad.

When *Senso* premiered at the Venice Film Festival in 1954, the Nazi occupation of Italy towards the end of World War II was a living memory. Indeed, at the time *Senso* could be understood as a near-allegory of the war years, with Austrian occupiers standing in for the Germans, the opportunistic Count Serpieri as the counterpart of the Fascist collaborator, and the patriotic Ussoni (a character Visconti added to the screen adaptation of the novel on which the film is based) as a leader in the mould of Communist resistance fighter. In a key scene cut from the film, the Italian commanders refuse Ussoni's impassioned offer to have the band of revolutionaries he leads fight alongside the regular army. Officials of the Italian army allied with the recently elected Christian Democrats demanded that the Ussoni scene be removed after a pre-release screening. The melodrama in this case may have cut a little too close to home, allegorically speaking, given that the PCI adopted a policy of cooperation rather than confrontation with other parties in the post-war period. After the parliamentary elections of 1948 put the centre-right Christian Democrats in power, with the PCI receiving only 31 per cent of the vote, the Communists were effectively excluded from government.[26] In other words, the deleted scene echoed recent Italian politics, with the army of Vittorio Emanuele's exclusion of Ussoni's patriotic forces from fighting prefiguring the Christian Democrats' exclusion of patriotic Communists from governing. The years immediately following World War II, with the abolition of the monarchy in 1946 and the 1948 elections, amounted to a kind of second founding of the nation of Italy. The scenario of *Senso* as Visconti intended it could be read as a critique of this second founding which, like the first, resulted not so much in revolution but in *trasformismo*, with things remaining the same despite political changes.[27]

The state censorship of *Senso* mandating deletion of the Ussoni scene and other seemingly arbitrary cuts had the unfortunate result of making Risorgimento history appear merely as a backdrop to the melodrama, whereas Visconti evidently meant for the melodrama to serve as a critique of the Risorgimento. In the censored version of the film, Risorgimento history – in this case the occupation of the Veneto region by Austro-Hungarian forces and its subsequent liberation, not by the Italian army but by Prussian forces who defeated the Austrians at the village of Sadowa (now in the Czech Republic) on 3 July 1866 – is hardly necessary to tell the story of a beautiful woman married to an older man who falls in love with a scoundrel who takes her money and leaves. That said, the melodramatic diegesis of the film as it exists today still manages to suggest that Risorgimento history itself was little more than melodrama, a meaning that would have been much more forceful had audiences been allowed to see the film that Visconti wanted them to see.

Visconti's next feature, *Le notti bianche* (*White Nights*, 1957), is often regarded as an interregnum in the director's career, a *sui generis* experiment in studio film-making that lies outside the twin tendencies of neorealism and historical melodrama followed thus far. The film is based on the Dostoevsky novella about a developing romance between a man and a woman who is despairing over a lost love; the would-be romance is cut short when the woman's lover returns at the last minute. In Visconti's telling, Dostoevsky's tortured romantics are transposed into the tortured neurotics Mario (Marcello Mastroianni), a minor clerk of some kind, and Natalia (Maria Schell), a seamstress who helps her blind grandmother repair Oriental rugs. Where *Bellissima* critiques commercial film-making, *White Nights* often seems to parody it. The combination of conventionality and incongruity notwithstanding, the film captures the characteristic tension between conflicting positions in Visconti's sensibility in an abstract, almost structuralist fashion. Here, the contrasts are drawn not between melodrama and history, as in *Senso*, or between fantasy and family, as in *Bellissima*, but between illusion and reality.[28] These two divergent modalities, however, are transposed at the end of the film, when the absent lover keeps his word and returns to Natalia, dashing the illusory hopes of Mario. The reversal occurs more at the level of the characters than of the audience, given that the long-absent lover is played by Jean Marais, who brings to the role the same oneiric formality he conveys in the films of Jean Cocteau, notably *La Belle et la Bête* (*Beauty and the Beast*, 1946). Marais' iconic presence aids the common interpretation of the film as a modern fairy tale, even though the terms *modern* and *fairy tale* serve as yet another expression of the conflicting, interpenetrating sensibilities that saturate the film.

With *Senso* and *White Nights*, Visconti's break with neorealism would seem to be complete. But his next film, *Rocco e i suoi fratelli* (*Rocco and His Brothers*, 1960), marks a partial return to the neorealist world that he had explored in *The Earth Trembles*. In fact, *Rocco and His Brothers* was originally conceived as a sequel that would follow the members of the Valastro family in *The Earth Trembles* on their journey from the impoverished South to the prosperous North. Even though Visconti abandoned the explicit link with his second feature (which survives in an early screenplay),[29] *Rocco and His Brothers* bears many of the hallmarks of neorealism, despite the professional casting featuring several non-Italian actors in key roles (which forced Visconti to abandon his usual preference for direct sound in favour of post-synchronisation for the dialogue). The film also carries forward the sensational melodrama of *Senso* while evoking the Southern Question that the Risorgimento failed to address. Of the five brothers – Vincenzo, Simone, Rocco, Ciro and Luca (whose names, in that order, serve as the titles of the five chapters, or acts, of the film) – two succeed in integrating themselves into the thriving economy of post-war Milan, Vincenzo (Spiros Focas) as a construction worker and Ciro (Max Cartier) as an assembly line worker at the Alfa Romeo factory. The youngest son, Luca (Rocco Vidolazzi), hopes to return to the southern homeland after which he is named, Lucania, an ancient region whose area spans parts of modern-day Basilicata and Calabria.[30] The film implies that Luca will indeed return to the South when he becomes a man, but one that will have been transformed by a modern industrial economy.

The emotional centre of the film, however, lies not with the successful sons but with Rocco (Alain Delon) and Simone (Renato Salvatori), who both fail – in different ways – to adapt to the economic miracle of Milan. But their failure follows from their adherence to certain positive values inculcated in the South – family loyalty above all – whereas the success of Vincenzo and Ciro entails an abandonment of those values. Socioeconomic integration comes at the cost of authenticity: such is the conundrum of modernity

that the southerner faces in the North. Rocco and Simone engage
in a *pas de deux* with destiny, with Simone's descent into depravity
paradoxically aided by the sacrifices the saintly Rocco makes to
support his brother. Simone follows the example of his elder brother
Vincenzo by becoming a professional boxer, but where Vincenzo
moved up from that profession, Simone moves down – blowing his
winnings on women and nightlife, getting so out of shape that he can
no longer compete in the ring, and finally surviving by petty theft
and borrowing money from his brothers. Rocco, likewise, goes into
boxing, first as Simone's sparring partner, but he soon shows himself
to be a more skilled athlete than his brother and wins a series of
matches. The melodramatic climax of the film comes when Rocco
fights for the European championship against a Swedish boxer and
wins, with the shots of Rocco's victory crosscut with shots of Simone
murdering the prostitute Nadia (Annie Giradot) with a switchblade.
Rocco is in the midst of his victory celebration when Simone comes
to the family flat and confesses to the murder, but only to Rocco, who
sobs uncontrollably, partly for Simone, but also for Nadia, whom
Rocco also loves. The film concludes with Luca saying goodbye to
Ciro at the Alfa Romeo plant, wandering past a newspaper kiosk
displaying Rocco's picture on the cover of a boxing magazine, then
walking down a street in a long closing shot accompanied by the
plaintive lyrics of Nino Rota's 'Paese mio' (My country).

The social and aesthetic worlds of *Rocco and His Brothers*
are well removed from those of *Senso*, with its decadent aristocratic
characters and sumptuous *mise en scène*. But the later film nonetheless
examines a different form of decadence by suggesting that modernity
itself, however progressive, produces a sick society, one where
integration into that society necessarily comes at a cost – the
disintegration of the traditional values of family and community,
no less. In a way, all the brothers – excepting Luca (whose destiny
lies outside the frame of the film) – wind up alienated from the life
that has formed them, albeit to different degrees, with Vincenzo
at one end of the social spectrum and Simone at the other, his fate

being the most melodramatically disastrous of all. Although *The Leopard* is often paired with *Senso* because of their shared focus on Risorgimento history, in many ways Visconti's second Risorgimento film has more in common with *Rocco and His Brothers*. Both appear to validate Gramsci's argument that Italian unification was a passive revolution, one that succeeded only for those already empowered while leaving the most disadvantaged behind. The two films approach the problem Gramsci identified not only from different historical vantage points, but also from different social positions. *The Leopard* shows how a powerful, aristocratic family maintained its power and prestige by accommodating and exploiting the social and political changes of the 1860s, while *Rocco and His Brothers* reveals the continuing effect of those changes on an impoverished peasant family in the 1960s. Together, the contrasting perspectives of the two films argue that however much things may have changed from one era to the next, ultimately they had remained the same.

3 The Production

The first day of the *Leopard* shoot was 14 March 1962. Visconti started with the Battle of Palermo, specifically the scene where a group of *picciotti* – young Sicilian men who had joined the fight with Garibaldi – are executed by a Bourbon firing squad. As was typical for action scenes throughout the film, Visconti had his cinematographer Giuseppe Rotunno set up three cameras to shoot from multiple angles and distances, giving the editor Mario Serandrei plenty of footage to work with. One detail of the battle scene that has become legendary as an example of Visconti's passion for authenticity concerns the Garabaldini's red-shirt uniforms, a mode of military dress that originated in 1843 when Garibaldi raised an army of Italian volunteers to fight in the Uruguayan Civil War and received a stockpile of red smocks from Montevideo originally meant for butchers.[31] Once the original stock ran out there was nothing uniform about the uniforms, since the soldiers dyed the shirts themselves, a detail Visconti took care to replicate by having his costume director Piero Tosi soak the shirts in tea and bake them in the sun, then distress them further by burying them underground to create an appropriately worn look.[32] The tailor Umberto Tirelli explains how a team of ten seamstresses worked independently of each other to ensure lack of uniformity in the design, together making some 300 shirts. Tosi did his shirt research at the Museo del Risorgimento in Palermo, where he also studied different types of Bourbon uniforms as well as the Garabaldini trousers, observing that they were very like today's blue jeans,[33] unsurprising given that modern jeans derive from the northern Italian fabric known as *bleu de Gênes* (Genoa blue, originally worn by sailors).[34]

Visconti likely began the shoot with the Battle of Palermo to get it out of the way early on, since it was easily the most challenging exterior scene in the film, its complexity matched only by the mostly interior ball segment at the end. All told, the full battle scene (shot in May) required some twenty professional actors plus 989 extras, who were a mixture of stuntmen recruited from Cinecittà and locals with little or no acting experience, including 170 children, the balance of adults assigned to play Garibaldini (375), bourgeois (30), commoners (240), Bourbon foot soldiers (120) and Bourbon cavalry (54). The latter were taught to ride by an army colonel who instructed them to sit upright with a straight back, nineteenth-century style, on stiff period saddles with long stirrups. All the Bourbon soldiers were played by Sicilians, whose dark complexions and short stature marked them off from the fairer, taller Garabaldini, most of whom were Cinecittà extras from Rome chosen for their northern look. Visconti filmed the main battle in the Piazza dello Spasimo, part of the old Arab quarter known as the Kalsa, although the city gate that the Redshirts storm through was constructed for the scene. Some of the rubble on the streets is real – damage left unrepaired after the allied bombing of Palermo in World War II.[35]

The allied bombing also played a role in the choice of location for the Salina Palace outside Palermo. Visconti's preference would have been the Palazzo Lampedusa, but the ancestral home of the Tomasi di Lampedusa had been destroyed by an American bomb in 1943. Visconti substituted the Villa Boscogrande just north of Palermo and had his set designer, the architect Mario Garbuglia, make the necessary repairs to the dilapidated villa. Garbuglia joked that the only parts of the estate he did not have to redo were the citrus grove, the air and the wind.[36] The renovations included a temporary addition to the structure to serve as the set for the Prince's observatory, an alteration made necessary because no room in the existing building was sufficiently elevated to provide the commanding view of the surrounding countryside the scene required. Visconti also recruited about twenty artists from Palermo and Rome to paint the ceiling frescoes for a brief flashback involving a visitor to the Salina estate who comes to view them.[37]

The observatory set under construction (courtesy Redazione Cappelli Editore, Bologna)

Garbuglia's architectural skills also came into play to create the Salina Palace in Donnafugata where the family go every summer to attend to their feudal holdings. The imaginary village of Donnafugata has its real-life counterpart in Palma di Montechiaro, about 150 km south of Palermo, while the Salina Palace in the fictional village was in Lampedusa's reality the Palazzo Filangeri di Cutò in Santa Margherita di Belice (108 km northwest of Palma and 73 km southwest of Palermo).[38] After the local mafia made it impossible for Visconti to shoot in Palma, his original preference,[39] location scouts found in the village of Ciminna, about 40 km southeast of Palermo, the perfect geographical counterpart of the Donnafugata described in the novel, with the Church of Saint Mary Magdalene adjacent to a large building that could serve in place of the Salina Palace. That building was derelict, so Garbuglia set about to completely restore the façade in nineteenth-century style and cover the existing modern paving of Piazza Matrice with rocks and pebbles hauled up on the backs of mules from the riverbed valley near the village. Only the restored

The Palazzo Filangeri
di Cutò, Lampedusa's
'Donnafugata', in
Santa Margherita
di Belice

The Donnafugata
palace façade in
Ciminna prior to
restoration (courtesy
Redazione Cappelli
Editore, Bologna); the
façade as it appears in
the film (below)

façade of the old building that had been transformed into the Salina Palace was suitable for filming, so the interior scenes at 'Donnafugata' were all shot at the vast Palazzo Chigi in Ariccia, near Rome. Lampedusa recalls that the Palazzo in Santa Margherita had some 300 rooms (to house twelve people),[40] and the Palazzo Chigi is of like dimensions, as we see in the long scene of Angelica and Tancredi chasing each other about through a seemingly endless series of rooms.

Of the three major locations in *The Leopard* – the Salina Palace in Palermo, the summer palace in Donnafugata and the Ponteleone Palace back in Palermo – only the last did not require restoration or reconstruction. The setting for the great ball put on by the Ponteleones is Palazzo Gangi, one of the few grand palaces in Sicily preserved intact (the owner could not say how many rooms the palace contained, but the camera crew scouting for the best locations estimated 218).[41] Hence, the focus of the production team was on the costumes and set dressing – the candles, the silverware and place settings, the food, the flowers. The August heat, even at night, compounded with the heat from the movie lights, made dealing with the candles almost a full-time job to keep them from going limp and replacing them when they did. Not content with the local flora, Visconti had flowers flown in regularly from San Remo in northern Italy; fifteen florists had been hired to deal with this aspect of the production. As for the food, ten cooks were engaged to ready the meals that appear in several scenes, including the vast outdoor supper, a feast that, depending on the number of takes, had to be prepared multiple times. At least one extra was fired for overeating, consuming so much food over the course of five rehearsals and three takes that the extra's appetite posed a continuity problem: 'Please remove yourself, young man,' Visconti ordered. 'I will not be able to match my shots. Already you are five pounds fatter than an hour ago.'[42]

Tosi and his assistants had to dress more than 350 actors and extras daily for the duration of the ball shoot, which went on for thirty-six days, mostly at night to mitigate the heat of the Sicilian summer. The ballgowns the women wear do not include the hoop skirts familiar from *Gone with the Wind* (1939) and other costume dramas set in the nineteenth century but were constructed out of multiple layers of different fabrics. The flare of Cardinale's dress, for example, results from no fewer than eleven tulle undergowns topped and held in place by an overskirt made of Dior organza (a type of stiff silk).[43] The women also wore foundation garments that were either original or copied from the period; Cardinale reported that her vintage corset was so tight it cut into her and made her waist bleed.[44] Visconti wanted as many real Sicilian aristocrats as possible to serve as extras, and he succeeded in recruiting roughly a third of the ball participants from actual nobility (including members of Lampedusa's extended family).[45] Several of these nobles provided possessions, such as china, cutlery, paintings, furniture and livery, for use as props. Some of the waiters in the scene (all professionals recruited from the local trade union) had trouble fitting into the authentic livery of the period, the increase in the average waistband no doubt attributable to Italy's economic miracle.

In addition to the many extras and technicians, the professional actors receiving screen credit numbered forty, most of the principals having worked with Visconti on other projects. The biggest European star at the time was undoubtedly Alain Delon, who had appeared in fourteen features prior to *The Leopard*, including Visconti's *Rocco and His Brothers*, Michelangelo Antonioni's *L'eclisse* (*The Eclipse*, 1962) and, of course, René Clément's *Plein soleil* (*Purple Noon*, 1960), the movie that made him a megastar. *The Leopard* was the twentieth feature for Claudia Cardinale, who had acted for Visconti before in *Rocco and His Brothers*. She was working on Federico Fellini's *8½* (1963) at the same time as the *Leopard* shoot, shuttling back and forth between Rome and Sicily and dyeing her hair from blonde (for Fellini) to brunette (for Visconti). Cardinale has provided insight into the different working methods of the two directors, Fellini being highly improvisational and Visconti much more formal and systematic, 'like theatre,' she said.[46] Indeed, the principal supporting actors (each given separate screen credit) had all worked with Visconti before in the theatre (he had directed more than thirty plays prior to *The Leopard*).

Rina Morelli, who plays Don Fabrizo's wife, Maria Stella, and Paolo Stoppa, who plays Don Calogero, were regulars in Visconti's theatre troupe. The married couple starred together multiple times under Visconti's direction, beginning in 1945 with Jean Anouilh's *Antigone* and Jean-Paul Sartre's *No Exit*. Their most recent collaboration with Visconti prior to *The Leopard* was in the short-lived drama *L'Arialda* from 1960, a play by Giovanni Testori that explored the Southern Question (shots from *Rocco and His Brothers* were projected as scenery) but was shut down by the censors because of references to homosexuality.[47] In 1952, Romolo Valli, who plays Father Pirrone, appeared with Morelli and Stoppa in a legendary staging at La Fenice in Venice of Carlo Goldoni's 1753 comedy *La locandiera* (*The Mistress of the Inn*), a production that also marked the beginning of Tosi's collaboration with Visconti as his costume designer. The casting of Valli, who had experience as both a stage actor and director of plays himself, confirms Cardinale's insight that the theatre played an outsize role in Visconti's attitude towards film performance in *The Leopard*.

Of the four supporting actors grouped together in the credits after the three principal ones who came to film from theatre, Mario Girotti must be singled out as a pure child of the movies (literally, since he had been a child actor) who had nothing to do with the stage. Girotti, who plays Count Cavriaghi, Tancredi's friend and fellow officer, later changed his name to Terence Hill and became one of the most bankable stars in the history of Italian cinema, making a string of highly successful comic parodies of Spaghetti Westerns, including … *continuavano a chiamarlo Trinità* (*Trinity is Still My Name*, 1971) in the *Trinity* franchise, for some time the highest-grossing Italian film ever, until it dropped in the rankings to fifth place.[48] With Lucilla Morlacchi, who portrays Salina's daughter Concetta, we revert to a performer with stage experience: she acted in the ill-fated *L'Arialda*, although her work in front of the camera both before and after *The Leopard* had been largely for television. Likewise, Pierre Clémenti had stage training and experience in his native France, but after his performance as Don Fabrizio's younger son Francesco Paolo in *The*

Leopard he went on to appear in several memorable art-house films by major directors, including Luis Buñuel's *Belle de jour* (1967) and Bernardo Bertolucci's *Il conformista* (*The Conformist*, 1970). Giuliano Gemma plays the Tuscan general who accompanies Tancredi to the Salina Palace to view the ceiling frescoes, a small role that seems incongruous with his credit placement. Like Girotti, Gemma was a pure product of the movie industry, having worked in one of the two most venerable Italian genres of a bygone era, the sword-and-sandal epic, prior to *The Leopard*, before going on afterwards to act in the other, the Spaghetti Western.

Most of the remaining actors given screen credit – including Ida Galli as Concetta's older sister Carolina and Ottavia Piccolo as her younger sister Caterina – barely have speaking roles. But the last three, each given separate screen credit, play critically important parts: Ivo Garrani as the voluble Colonel Pallavicino, Leslie French as the earnest Cavaliere Chevalley and Serge Reggiani as the loyal but aggrieved Ciccio Tumeo. Garrani was yet another stage actor who gravitated to film, but his work on *The Leopard* did not exactly vault him into elite roles with other major directors (as happened with Clémenti). For example, he worked in Italian horror films like *Seddok, l'erede di Satana* (*Atom Age Vampire*, 1960) pre-Visconti and *Zora la vampira* (*Zora the Vampire*, 2000) post-Visconti. The British actor French, by contrast, was one of the most accomplished stage performers of his generation, making a name for himself at London's Old Vic Theatre as a Shakespearean actor (after *The Leopard*, Visconti cast him in the minor role as a travel agent in *Morte a Venezia* (*Death in Venice*, 1971)). The Franco-Italian Reggiani had a remarkable career in France as both an acclaimed film actor and a renowned singer, his versatility perhaps contributing to his interpretation of Don Ciccio, whose divergent roles as church organist and the Prince's hunting companion call for a like adaptability.

The casting of Burt Lancaster in the title role threatened to poison the production from the very beginning, since Goffredo Lombardo, head of the production company Titanus, had made the decision to give Lancaster the lead without consulting Visconti. The practice of enlisting major American stars for leading roles in Italian films (such as Farley Granger in *Senso*) was common at the time. The strategy was adopted to ensure profitable box-office receipts because the Hollywood studio that 'owned' the star, in this case 20th Century-Fox, would underwrite a portion of the production costs. Visconti's preference for the lead was, first, Nikolay Cherkasov, star of Sergei Eisenstein's *Aleksandr Nevski* (*Alexander Nevsky*, 1938), then Marlon Brando, and finally Lawrence Olivier, none of whom were available. But the deal Lombardo made meant that Fox had a say in which actors were available for loan to Titanus, which turned out to be Gregory Peck, Anthony Quinn, Spencer Tracy or Lancaster. Visconti wanted to interview each of the actors, but Lombardo went ahead and hired Lancaster and informed the director after the fact. From Lombardo's perspective, the American star must have seemed like a sure thing, since Lancaster was at the height of his considerable celebrity in the early 1960s, having received a Best Actor Academy Award for *Elmer Gantry* (1960) and another nomination for *Birdman of Alcatraz* (1962).[49]

Visconti was not pleased. He thought of Lancaster as a 'cowboy' or a 'gangster', despite the actor's recent turn away from roles that might have justified such epithets. But Lancaster immersed himself in the part of the Prince, reading and rereading the Lampedusa novel; researching the history of the Risorgimento; spending time with Lampedusa's widow and his adopted son Gioacchino Lanza Tomasi (who also advised Visconti); and cultivating relationships with Sicilian nobility in order to better understand how to play an old-world aristocrat who knows his class is in decline.[50] He soon realised, however, that the model for the character he was asked to play was right in front of him – Visconti. Lancaster arrived in Sicily in mid-May 1962 and quickly won over his fellow actors, partly by suggesting that all of them act in their own language instead of English, as Lancaster's contract stipulated. By contrast, it was not until August that Visconti finally accepted the American, but only after Lancaster exploded in anger over the director's disdainful treatment of him. Following the outburst, Visconti's long-time screenwriter Suso Cecchi d'Amico says that the two became friends, almost like brothers: 'Real, deep affection, esteem, respect, solidarity – but not closeness.' By 2 November, their mutual birthday (Lancaster turned forty-nine, Visconti fifty-six), they had developed such rapport and become so familiar with one another's tastes that they unknowingly gave each other the same gift – paintings by the politician-cum-artist Renato Guttuso.[51]

During the shoot Lancaster told a reporter that Visconti was 'far and away the best director I've ever worked with', adding, 'I've never seen a director rehearse so thoroughly. No detail escapes him.' The example he gives is of Visconti personally stuffing the mattress the Prince and Princess lie on in the scene where the two argue over Tancredi's choice of Angelica over Concetta: 'The mattress isn't even on camera, but that didn't stop Luchino. Its lumpiness would help the scene.'[52] Another example: for the opening scene of the family saying the rosary together, Visconti directed Lancaster to go to a dresser and take a handkerchief from a drawer (evidently the one the Prince kneels on during prayers). When he did so, he found that the dresser was 'fully stocked with a fine array of princely regalia – 20 custom made shirts, 15 pairs of handwoven socks, 30 cravats and more than a dozen handkerchiefs', none of which appear on camera.[53] These types of anecdotes – and there are many – reveal the method in Visconti's madness for authenticity. Whether that method has its roots in Konstantin Stanislavsky's is complicated by Visconti's ambiguous attitude towards the Russian dramaturge,[54] but the two methods have in common an effort to get the actor to experience rather than simply perform a role. The difference, perhaps, resides more in means than ends. Whereas the Stanislavsky disciple Lee Strasberg relied on psychological means ('emotional memory', or some such) to help the actor experience genuine feelings,[55] Visconti entrusted the effect he wanted to more materialistic devices by making the physical *mise en scène* critical to the actor's capacity for experience. The key to Visconti's direction, in other words, is production.

4 The Film

The Leopard opens with a title sequence of roughly three minutes, accompanied by music from Nino Rota's then-unfinished *Sinfonia sopra una canzone d'amore* (Symphony on a love song),[56] that draws the audience closer and closer to a great estate sitting in a lush plane amid arid, white mountains. Extreme long shots of the mansion and the grounds surrounding it include closer shots of a weather-worn bust, its features broken and decayed, making it unidentifiable except as a marble emblem of the deteriorated state of the aristocratic family we are shortly to meet. Moving ever closer to the building, the establishing shots give way to a pan past the side of the structure, showing its window balcony doors open and the wind fluttering the curtains. The music fades and mixes with the muttering sounds of the rosary, as the camera finally introduces us to the inhabitants of the place: an assortment of elegantly dressed men and women, all young, as well as a few children, along with an older woman and an extraordinarily dignified older man, who tells his rosary beads and follows the prayer from a book lying open in the seat of the

Establishing decay

chair before which he kneels. The worshippers are distracted by shouts outside the room, prompting one of the young men to rise, but another young man pulls him back – action which a manservant takes as a signal that he should be the one to leave the room and investigate. The priest, distracted, winds down the service, his voice trailing off until the patriarch of the place snaps his prayer book shut, rises and slowly folds the large, brocaded handkerchief on which he had been kneeling.

Unlike *Senso*, the opening credits of *The Leopard* offer no information about the time and place of the action before us. In fact, absent an extraordinary knowledge of geography, the uninitiated viewer has no way of knowing that the landscape is that of Sicily. The *mise en scène* of a morning mass in a private chapel, however, pretty clearly pegs the scene to sometime in the nineteenth century. But we do not know precisely when or where we are until the servant returns with a letter and a newspaper that he presents to the patriarch, after first conveying the disturbing news that a dead soldier has been found in the garden. The patriarch reads the letter first and learns that General Garibaldi has landed at Marsala with an army of 800 men. Now we know that we are in the Sicilian countryside on a day in the middle of May in 1860: the revolutionary moment of the Risorgimento has arrived. Where the audience for *Senso* had the historical information spelled out for them beforehand, the audience for *The Leopard* experiences the history much as the characters in the film do: it dawns on them gradually and confusedly, not by means of non-diegetic language on the screen but through the details of the diegesis itself. Visconti's modification in the method whereby cinema is made to represent history likely lies in his deepening understanding of Hungarian Marxist Georg Lukács's theories of literary realism, especially *The Historical Novel* (1937).[57] There, Lukács credits Balzac with a key insight about the significance of Sir Walter Scott's historical novels: that they represent historical figures 'as history itself had done when it required their appearance. The reader, therefore, experiences the historical genesis of the important historical figures, and it is the writer's task from then on to let their actions make them appear the real representatives of these historical crises.'[58]

The sense of crisis is key, for Lukács understood 'human progress' as the product of 'the inner conflict of social forces in history itself' (p. 27). Moreover, the historical novelist was expected to be not just a passive recorder of social crises and conflicts but a critical analyst of them. Only by means of a critical consciousness could the novelist hope to offer 'a ruthlessly truthful investigation and disclosure of all the contradictions of progress' (p. 29) and reveal thereby 'a clear understanding of history as a process, of history as the concrete precondition of the present' (p. 21). In Visconti's case, his reading of Gramsci informed the critical consciousness brought to bear on Risorgimento history, but that consciousness was also informed by the present itself, the contradictions of which Visconti had ruthlessly investigated in *Rocco and His Brothers*. Having treated revolutionary history as melodrama in *Senso*, Visconti developed a critical awareness of the impact of that earlier history on the present in *Rocco and His Brothers*, then returned to it in *The Leopard* with a fuller understanding of 'history as the concrete precondition of the present'. The relevance of Lukács to Visconti's treatment of history in *The Leopard* is further confirmed by Lukács's comment in his preface to the English translation of *The Historical Novel* that certain 'new important historical novels, like ... Lampedusa's *The Leopard* (particularly its first half) confirm the principles I arrived at in a positive direction' (p. 14).[59]

The Prince retires to a small sitting room to read the news of Garibaldi's invasion to his family: his wife Maria Stella, his elder son Paolo, his younger son Francesco Paolo and his three daughters – Carolina (the oldest), Concetta and Caterina (the youngest).[60] The news sends Princess Maria Stella into hysterics, but the Prince himself remains commanding and calm. He announces that dinner will be in half an hour, after which he will depart for Palermo, accompanied by Father Pirrone. Next, the film cuts to an advancing shot of the dead soldier mentioned in the previous scene, identifiable by his uniform

Family group in an interior: (from left) Paolo, Caterina, Prince Fabrizio, Francesco Paolo, Princess Maria Stella, Carolina, Concetta

as a royalist, lying beneath a lemon tree. Several servants stand about the body as the gardener says, 'These swine smell even worse when they are dead',[61] evidently before he notices the approaching Prince. The gardener then takes off his hat and bows, explaining that the dead man's regiment has been notified and that someone will come to take the body away. As the camera moves ever closer to the body, one of the workmen uses his handkerchief to cover the face of the corpse, and the brief scene ends. Because it is shot from the point of view of the Prince (as we know from the gardener's greeting and the

The dead Bourbon soldier from the Prince's POV

deferential behaviour of the other workmen), there is considerable irony in the disrespect shown towards the dead soldier – the crack about the odour of the body – and the respect accorded to Salina, since his aristocratic power descends from the same Bourbon king the soldier served.

The following segment shows Salina and Father Pirrone seated in the carriage the Prince ordered so commandingly. We might assume from the urgency of the earlier scene that the Prince is on his way to attend to the security of his villa in the city, or to some other important matter related to the impending presence of Garibaldi's Redshirts. But no: Salina travels to visit his mistress (or favourite prostitute), with the priest on board as the beard. The carriage is forced to stop at a checkpoint guarded by Bourbon soldiers (identifiable as such by the same uniform we have already seen on the dead soldier), but they quickly recognise the Prince and allow him to pass. The Prince is completely unperturbed by this momentary inconvenience, remaining confident in his prestige and authority despite the politically perilous times. Father Pirrone says something about how the Prince's nephew Tancredi needs to be more careful about the company he keeps, but Salina cuts him short. After the carriage passes through the checkpoint, the priest remarks, 'What a beautiful country this would be if—' and the Prince interrupts: 'if there weren't so many Jesuits.' As here, scenes involving the Prince and the priest are often comic, with Father Pirrone seeming a bit like a court jester or a fool in a Shakespeare play. The comic contrast continues when the Prince drops the priest off at a chapel, wishing him 'good prayers' before heading for the brothel. Once there he is warmly welcomed by a fleshy woman – not that young – who addresses him with an augmentative suffix, calling him 'Principone' ('big Prince' – a pet name with sexual connotations).

Having been 'introduced' to Tancredi Falconeri by the busybody priest, we now meet the man in person when his face appears reflected in the Prince's shaving mirror. Visconti had shown himself to be adept at this type of skilled camerawork in earlier films,

A reflection on Sicilian nobility

but here the mirror shot is much more than mere cinematic virtuosity; rather, it emphasises the Prince's connection to his beloved nephew. The Prince sees in Tancredi a reflection of his younger self: both possess the privilege and prestige, as well as the sense of worldliness and sophistication, common to their class. But there the resemblance ends: Don Fabrizio is a scion of the noble past, Tancredi a man of the bourgeois future. After a bit of banter about his uncle's erotic exploits the night before, Tancredi explains that he has decided to join the revolution and become a Garibaldino. At first, Salina is incredulous, until Tancredi delivers the famous line: 'If we want things to stay as they are, things will have to change' (p. 28). The words have a profound effect on Salina: he had not considered that the revolution might be manipulated to the advantage of his own class and is impressed that Tancredi has made precisely that calculation. Having broken the news to his uncle, Tancredi proceeds to say goodbye to the household, accompanied by Bendicò, the huge Great Dane that Lampedusa called 'a vitally important character and practically the key to the novel'.[62] Although the dog's role as a symbol of the deteriorating aristocracy (the animal winds up as a rug) is less pronounced in the film, the creature does appear in any number of key scenes (despite being the most difficult 'actor' in the film),[63] suggesting that Visconti was keen to signal the class connotations of the Leopard's faithful canine companion. Tancredi's goodbyes include a quiet moment with Concetta, who at this point appears destined to marry her cousin.

With Tancredi gone, the Prince retires to his observatory (see p. 12), accompanied by Father Pirrone. This scene complements the earlier one with Tancredi and covers some of the same material from a different perspective. Before, where Tancredi ribbed his uncle for his libertine behaviour, the priest condemns it as sinful and urges the Prince to make a formal confession. Now, it is the Prince who explains that the revolution is nothing more than a transformation, 'an imperceptible substitution of classes'. A key detail of the set is the array of telescopes and the double stack of books and journals, establishing the Prince's scientific interest in astronomy. The historical figure on whom Lampedusa based his novel was an amateur astronomer who made some real discoveries and published his findings in scientific journals, and the character in the novel often reflects on the heavenly indifference to human affairs the distant stars convey. This aspect of the character comes through in Lancaster's lofty bearing, his portrayal of a man who finds the workings of this world – including his own destiny – as somehow beneath him.

The Prince's aloof perspective carries over into Visconti's staging of the battle scene between Garibaldi's forces and the

More Garabaldini than Borbonici

Tancredi at war

Bourbon army at Palermo. A ground level shot shows the Redshirts
storming through one of the city gates, the flag bearer waving the
Italian tricolour. A crane shot follows, capturing the scale of the
assault, with many more revolutionary than royalist forces seen
in this and most other shots. The camera sometimes travels with
the advancing soldiers in the main battle, often cutting to smaller
skirmishes in what amounts to urban warfare. But we never get
to 'know' the combatants – on either side – through close-ups or
reverse angle shots. Near the end of the battle, we finally see Tancredi
in a medium shot, the closest shot of any figure in the segment.
Significantly, he is not wearing the homemade red-shirt 'uniform' of
the Garibaldini, only a faded red kerchief knotted about his neck.
Tancredi may be dressed as a civilian, but he is in a position of
authority. Earlier, we have seen a few armed civilians mixed in with
the Redshirts, but Tancredi leads a group of them. When an explosion
knocks him to the ground, he staggers to his feet and shelters by a
wall before placing a hand on his wounded head and running to a
convent, where he finds sanctuary with other soldiers. The segment
ends with billowing white smoke from the battle that covers the
dissolve to the next segment: the Salina family's journey to their
estate in Donnafugata.

The 'wagon train' to Donnafugata

The advantages of the widescreen format are impressively evident in the several extreme long shots of the caravan of carriages making its way through the parched landscape. The long shots are reminiscent of John Ford and the Hollywood Western (the carriages look very like a wagon train), a genre that was in decline in the US at the time *The Leopard* was made. As the camera follows the carriages through the countryside, the Western element is enhanced by shots of Tancredi on horseback riding alongside the caravan, sometimes leading it. Suddenly, the train of carriages encounters a roadblock manned by Garibaldini, who have orders to prevent anyone from

No peasants allowed

passing, even those civilians with valid papers issued by the new authorities. Tancredi takes charge, identifying himself as a military captain (though he is in civilian dress) who fought with Garibaldi's forces at Palermo, and, wielding his riding crop like a sword, orders the soldiers to let the carriages pass. His orders are obeyed, but the soldiers quickly close the blockade again to prevent the passage of those behind the Salina family. The screenplay underlines the injustice of letting the aristocrats pass while the commoners are forced to wait: 'If others pass, why not us too? Where's the justice in that?' This is the second time the Prince has successfully made it through a military roadblock – the first royalist, the second republican – actions that argue in favour of *trasformismo*: nothing has changed, despite the changes.

The theme of *trasformismo* is picked up in the next scene, set in a rustic roadside inn, as the camera pans from Tancredi sleeping on a bed of straw to a group of peasants at table with Father Pirrone. 'You live among the nobles, what do the lords say about all this, this great conflagration?,' one peasant asks. 'What does Prince Salina say about it?' 'They're different,' explains the priest, and care about different things from ordinary people. 'If you ask him what he thinks of the revolution,' Father Pirrone explains, 'he says that there has been no revolution and that everything will continue as before.' The peasant agrees, whereupon Father Pirrone opens his Bible and starts to read from Psalm 44. This psalm is sometimes called the martyr's prayer because it expresses lamentation over abandonment by God for allowing the enemies of the faithful to prosper. Father Pirrone reads aloud in Latin, so his auditors do not understand that, allegorically speaking, he has put himself in the position of devoted royalist mourning the end of the Bourbon regime. The psalm aside, Father Pirrone's monologue is lifted almost verbatim from the unfilmed chapter of the novel about the priest's visit to his home village of San Cono. In the midst of Father Pirrone's reading, the camera picks up a young woman carrying a bucket and follows her through the room, out of an interior door to another room and up

Cinematography by Caravaggio

a flight of stairs. A cut shows her walking towards the camera in a scene that has no relation to the story (aside from the noble presence of Bendicò), but the shot is so beautifully composed and lit that it looks like a Caravaggio painting, an intended reference, according to the cinematographer Rotunno.[64]

This painterly quality continues in the following scene when the screen is once again filled with white, an effect similar to that of the billowing white smoke that formed the transition from the scene of battle to the journey to Donnafugata. This time, the mass of whiteness is quickly revealed to be a large sheet being spread upon the ground by the servants for a luncheon on the grass, Caravaggio having given way to Manet (see p. 100). During this lunch, the Prince holds forth to one of the local peasants. Sitting on a tree stump that looks like a rustic throne, he begins to explain the revolutionary state of affairs from his perspective: his words take visual form when a dissolve delivers us back to the Salina Palace near Palermo, where the Prince receives Tancredi, now red-shirted as an officer in the Garibaldian army, along with his commanding officer – a general – and another soldier, Tancredi's friend Count Cavriaghi, all of whom salute the Prince. This is another first-person scene like the one earlier with the dead Bourbon soldier, except that in this one we hear the Prince speaking to his guests, the voiceover approximating the free

Remembrance of things past; Garabaldini from the Prince's POV; *Il gattopardo rampante al fresco*

indirect discourse of Lampedusa's novel, which is mostly limited to the point of view of Salina. Tancredi looks back at his unseen uncle and comments that the general has violated Garibaldi's first revolutionary rule by calling the Prince 'Eccellenza'. The general is a Tuscan who has come to the palace to view the ceiling frescoes, which include the family crest, featuring the heraldic symbol of il gattopardo.

The flashback is suspended and we return to the present: lunch is done and we see Tancredi being unusually attentive to Concetta. (Earlier, he helped cool her face with water from a trough – before doing the same for his horse, which perhaps says something about his true feelings for his cousin.) This action is covered by the sounds of the Tuscan general singing a tenor aria from Vincenzo Bellini's La sonnambula (The Sleepwalker, 1831), as we return to the flashback. Bellini was a Sicilian composer, so the selection is an act of homage by the general to his hosts. The operatic context of the aria he sings is an expression of the character Rodolfo's nostalgia for his native village, which he sees again after a long absence: 'Vi ravviso, o luoghi ameni' (I see you again, oh lovely scenes). The diegetic context is quite ironic, since the general first saw the 'lovely scenes' of Sicily when he helped to conquer them. The performance of an aria from an opera about a sleepwalker also includes a comic dimension, as Father Pirrone and the Princess nod off, and even Bendicò yawns.

The flashback contrasts sharply with the next scene, which opens with the oom-pah-pah sounds of the village band in Donnafugata warming up to play the gypsy girl's song from Act II of Verdi's La traviata as part of the welcoming ceremony for the Salina family. The juxtaposition of the Tuscan general's refined singing and the village band's earnest mutilation of Verdi reveals the stark difference between the sophistication of the North and the simplicity of the South. The band plays in front of the graffito slogan 'Viva Garibaldo' (evidently a dialectical variation on 'Viva Garibaldi').[65] An earlier shot shows the villagers passing by another graffito message as they rush to greet the Salina family: 'Viva re Vittorio',

Welcome to Donnafugata

which, together with the tune from *La traviata*, is a reminder of how thoroughly nationalised the music of Verdi had become during the Risorgimento (his name was read as an acronym for 'Vittorio Emanuele, Re D'Italia').

When the carriages bearing the Salina family stop in front of the impressive façade of the palace (see p. 37), the Prince is the first to step out of the coach, whereupon he is welcomed by an assortment of villagers who, despite the revolution, continue to behave like the loyal subjects they have been all their lives. These include Don Calogero Sedàra, the mayor of the village (wearing a tricolour sash), and Don Ciccio Tumeo, the Prince's hunting partner, who has brought along a favourite pointer bitch. Don Ciccio is also the church organist, so he rushes off to perform in the next stage of the traditional welcoming for the family to their summer estate. As the band continues to play the gypsy tune from *La traviata* outside the church, Don Ciccio coaxes the organ inside to emit the strains of 'Amami, Alfredo' (Love me, Alfredo) from the same opera, the aria that the dying Violetta sings to her lover assuring him that her love will last beyond the grave. This is a strange choice of musical prelude to the traditional Te Deum, the prayer of public rejoicing that, in this case, celebrates the Salina family's arrival, but Visconti's inclusion of the music follows the novel, one of many possible examples of how faithful the director was to his source.

A deity; the first signs of the death of a class

Visconti cuts from a long overhead shot of the dignified procession into the church (with the revolutionary graffito 'Viva Garibaldo' visible on the wall through the open door) to a slow, close pan of the stucco sculpture overlooking the altar. The shot moves down to the ornately garbed backs of clerics before the altar, then cuts to a slow tracking shot showing the members of the Salina family seated in the choir stalls, grey and dusty from the long carriage ride to Donnafugata. They appear not so different from the mostly monochrome sculptural figures we have just seen; in fact, the look is rather cadaverous, oddly congruent with the Verdi aria about impending death. Archibald Colquhoun recalls how Visconti used a bellows to cover his actors with talcum powder for the scene and muttered 'death, death' as he did so, adding, 'This symbolizes the first signs of the death of a class!'[66]

The next scene begins with the Prince luxuriating in a bath after the long, dusty journey from Palermo. The bath is interrupted when a servant announces that Father Pirrone needs to see the Prince on an urgent matter. Irritated, Salina rises naked (looking like the Farnese Hercules, Lampedusa says) as the priest enters, the occasion for some comic business about how embarrassed the cleric is to see a naked body when he has seen so many naked souls. Father Pirrone has come to the Prince to tell him that Concetta is in love, but the Prince cuts him off before he can say with whom – the Prince knows that it is Tancredi. He also knows how inappropriate such a union would be, given the brilliant political future the Prince foresees for his nephew and the inadequate dowry that Concetta would confer on the marriage. In Catholic theology, the priest is the mediator between God and man, who needs the priest's intercession in the care of the soul. Here, the priest appears in the role of secular mediator between Concetta and the Prince, which casts Salina in the role of God. Visconti's camera appears to confirm this reading as the scene concludes, with the Prince taking tripartite form, standing in a room reflected in two mirrors. This 'Trinitarian' treatment makes a certain

Trinitarian reflections

amount of sense, given that the patriarch Salina more than fulfils
the role of Father, while his unseen but commanding influence over
his feudal dominions suggests the Holy Ghost. Moreover, Tancredi,
Salina's 'son' fathered by another man, completes the Trinity,
especially since we have already seen the 'father' reflected as the 'son'
in that earlier mirror shot.

The question of Concetta's love having been dismissed, the
Prince attends to the more important business of dressing for
luncheon with the locals and their wives. The family is assembled with
a number of guests in a sumptuous sitting room when the mayor's
arrival is announced. He is wearing evening clothes – for an afternoon
luncheon – as we see in a shot of Don Calogero from the Prince's
point of view from atop a flight of stairs, the downward perspective
emphasising the social heights the Prince occupies. The ill-fitting
evening dress is the first of a succession of faux pas – the mayor tries
to shake hands with the Prince, he brings his uninvited daughter
instead of his wife, he gulps down a full glass of wine at dinner instead
of sipping it, and so on – all of which illustrate that new political
equality is no match for old social distinctions. But the prestige of the
old regime is suddenly faced with a different kind of challenge –
or a different kind of opportunity – when the bourgeois mayor's
beautiful daughter Angelica arrives. Her presence is 'announced' first

Rube ascending a staircase

Concetta assesses the competition; Angelica arrives

by Concetta's stricken look, then by Tancredi's astonished gaze, before the viewer sees her. A series of reaction shots follow: the Prince's startled expression; Father Pirrone's embarrassed glance; and, most interesting of all, Don Ciccio's knowing shrug, as if to say, 'What would you expect?' (as we later learn, he is one of the few people who has seen Don Calogero's beautiful but reclusive wife). Angelica may be as overdressed for the occasion as her bumptious father, but she is all elegance as she glides across the room – past the Prince and past Tancredi (who bends as if to greet her before she moves on). Angelica knows the social protocols: she goes to the Princess first, then to the Prince, then Concetta and finally to Tancredi – but she waits for her father to introduce her. Tancredi almost violates social convention by leaning forward to kiss Angelica's hand, but she maintains the poise that prevents such a premature gesture of affection.

The family and their guests sit down for the luncheon in a room saturated with aristocratic finery: paintings and gilded candle sconces adorn the walls, with silver candelabra, crystal and china on the table. To the relief of everyone, the meal does not begin with soup, but with macaroni, which, despite the name, is a far cry from the familiar pasta dish known as 'macaroni and cheese'. Here, we need the supplement of the novel to explain that the dish is in keeping with the sumptuousness of the setting in which it is served:

Luncheon is served; macaroni, Sicilian style

[T]he appearance of those monumental dishes of macaroni was worthy of the quivers of admiration they evoked. The burnished gold of the crusts, the fragrance of the sugar and cinnamon they exuded, were but preludes to the delights released from the interior when the knife broke the crust; first came a mist laden with aromas, then chicken livers, hard-boiled eggs, sliced ham, chicken, and truffles in masses of piping hot, glistening macaroni, to which the meat juice gave an exquisite hue of suede. (p. 79)

This 'macaroni', in other words, is really the Italian dish called either *timballo* or *timpano* because of its drum-like shape.

Aside from the macaroni, the star of the meal is Tancredi, who sits between Angelica and Concetta and regales the table with war stories, notably the tale of breaking into the Benedictine convent at Piazza Origlione in Palermo to establish a lookout post at the top of the building. When the soldiers finally succeed in battering the door open, the aged nuns in their black habits scream and try to hide from the band of young Garibaldini, until one of Tancredi's comrades explains that they need not fear: 'Nothing doing, sisters, we've got other things to think of; but we'll be back when you've got some novices.' It is obvious from his reaction that the Prince thinks the story is inappropriate, and even Tancredi appears embarrassed, but Angelica is riveted. She says, admiringly, that she wishes she had

Angelica gets the joke

The happy couple

been there with him to see for herself. 'Had you been there,' Tancredi replies, 'we'd have had no need to wait for novices' (p. 82). Far from being offended, Angelica is delighted: she finds Tancredi's remark hilarious and laughs, uncontrollably, for a good thirty seconds. She is still laughing when the Prince, indignant, rises as a signal that the meal has ended, at which point the prudish Concetta confronts Tancredi and tells him that his story would have been better told to his confessor, 'not to young ladies at table; or at least not when I'm there' (p. 83). The reverse angle shows Tancredi and Angelica in a medium two-shot: this is the moment they become a couple. *The Leopard* does not have a conventional plot, but if it did, this would be the climax – the point where the declining aristocracy and the rising bourgeoisie form a union to the mutual advantage of each class. The alliance of the two classes foretold by Tancredi's vulgar story and Angelica's vulgar response begins to take shape when the Prince looks down from a palace balcony on his nephew, dressed in top hat and frock coat and trailed by a servant bearing a basket of what look to be oranges (the novel says peaches), heading for the Sedàra household. The Prince is amused but says to himself that he will support Tancredi's romantic ambitions, even though they are 'a touch ignoble'.

A cut shows a weathered statue kitted out with the tricolour banner before the camera dollies down to a young Sicilian man, singing an a cappella version of 'La bella Gigogin', a patriotic song composed in 1858 originally in Piedmontese dialect that casts the amours of a young girl ('Gigogin' is a diminutive of 'Teresa' in Piedmontese) as a political allegory: her leaving her husband stands in for the Austrians leaving Lombardia when the Italians drove them out.[67] Here, the allegory has been adapted for the Sicilian context – and dialect ('Gigogin' becomes 'Gigugin') – with Bourbons in place of Austrians. The camera tracks right to left along a row of young men, all wearing hats with cards reading 'Si' tucked into their hatbands, singing the chorus of the song: 'Dàghela avanti un passo, / delizia del mio cuore!' (Take a step forward, / delight of my heart!). The day is 22 October 1860, the date of the plebiscite giving the inhabitants of the Italian peninsula the opportunity to vote to become citizens of the nation-state of Italy – or to remain subjects of a royalist regime. The Prince and Father Pirrone walk through a duststorm to the village hall, with signs reading 'Viva il plebiscito' and 'SI All'Italia unita' plastered on the walls. As they enter, everyone doffs their hats to the Prince, who turns aside and calls the mayor 'the Cavour of Donnafugata' – an ironic compliment, since the mayor is hardly the equivalent of the conservative nobleman Camillo Benso, Count of Cavour, who became unified Italy's first Prime Minister. The vote is scarcely secret: the mayor holds two cards, 'Si' and 'No'; the Prince chooses 'Si' and strikes the top of the ballot box decisively as he drops the card through the slot. After the Prince votes, the mayor calls a temporary halt to the proceedings for patriotic refreshments in his office, adorned with portraits of Vittorio Emanuele and Garibaldi. The mayor produces a platter with neatly arranged glasses of tricolour liqueurs – red, green and white. When the Prince picks white, someone interprets the choice as one final gesture of Bourbon sympathy, a remark that makes the mayor wince.

That evening, the townspeople assemble in the square below the mayor's villa to hear him read the results of the plebiscite from his balcony, decorated with candles in tricolour glasses. The scene is comic: the band strikes up prematurely and the wind blows the candles out, the sudden lack of light making it difficult for the mayor to read his patriotic declaration and announce the vote: of 515 registered voters, 512 voted 'Sí', with zero voting 'No'. The Prince is watching the ceremony as well, and since the Salina Palace is directly across from the Sedàra villa, he and Angelica exchange greetings from their respective balconies. Finally, the ceremony concludes with red, white and green fireworks bursting in the night sky.

The pyrotechnic display contrasts sharply with the next shot: a full moon, serene at dawn, a visual reminder that however much the country may have changed, the countryside remains the same. That sentiment is shortly to be echoed by the Prince, who strides beneath the dawn moon through the hills outside Donnafugata, hunting rabbits with his loyal retainer, Don Ciccio. The pair do shoot a few rabbits and woodcocks, but the hunting trip is mainly an excuse for the Prince to get information about the Sedàras from Don Ciccio, who has a lot to say when the hunters pause for lunch. He explodes with royalist anger over the plebiscite, in which he voted 'No', but the mayor changed it to 'Sí', turning Don Ciccio, as he puts it, from a 'faithful subject' to a 'filthy pro-Bourbon' (p. 113). The dialogue in this scene is lifted largely from the novel, but Visconti could not make explicit the long-term ramifications of the indignity and injustice visited on people like Don Ciccio, which Lampedusa's

A rustic lunch

Visconti makes a point to Lancaster as Reggiani looks on

omniscience allows in the passage diagnosing the cause of the problems the people of the South face as 'the stupid annulment of the first expression of liberty ever offered them' (p. 113). The best Don Fabrizio can do to soothe his retainer's political wounds is explain that, after all, one monarch has been exchanged for another, with the Bourbons giving way to the House of Savoy. The plebiscite, he says, was a necessary evil: 'Something had to change for everything to stay as it was.'

Moving on from politics, the Prince wants to know more about Don Calogero's personal life, and Don Ciccio obliges. He tells the Prince that the mayor's miserly habits and devilish cleverness have led to the accumulation of enormous wealth. Moreover, recent political developments position him to purchase Church property at a pittance in the coming years, a prophecy that confirms fears earlier expressed by Father Pirrone. He also informs the Prince about Donna Bastiana, Sedàra's beautiful but illiterate wife (not only can she not read, she cannot tell time by the clock), who is rarely seen in public, aside from the 5.00 am mass – which is where Don Ciccio, hiding behind a confessional, got a good look at her. Donna Bastiana is the daughter of Peppe Giunta, a peasant so dirty and disgusting everyone called him Peppe 'Mmerda.

These squalid stories about the backgrounds of the Prince's future in-laws cue a flashback to the night before: lying in bed, the Princess goes into outraged hysterics over Tancredi's 'deception' of Concetta with that 'slut' Angelica. The Prince assures his wife that Angelica is not a slut – though she might one day become one; for now, she's just a young girl trying to make a good marriage. The cut back to the conclusion of the hunting scene reveals Don Ciccio to be as outraged over the prospective marriage as the Princess is. The Prince becomes so angry that he threatens to strike Don Ciccio, before verbalising what in the novel are presented as his thoughts: 'This marriage is not the end of everything, but the beginning of everything. It is in the very best of traditions.' Knowing Don Ciccio's reputation for gossip, the Prince makes him pay the price of knowing that he plans to ask Sedàra for Angelica's hand on behalf of his nephew: Don Ciccio will be locked in the gunroom with the dogs until the marriage negotiations are concluded. The pair then head down the mountain for the village. In the novel, Lampedusa writes, 'And as they climbed down the road, it would have been difficult to tell which of the two was Don Quixote and which was Sancho Panza' (p. 121), the politics of the age rendering the boundaries of reality and illusion more uncertain than ever.

Lampedusa describes the embarrassing necessity of the Prince's negotiating with the clever but repugnant Sedàra as 'eating a toad' (p. 89). The words are not used in the film, but Lancaster's expression at different points in the scene suggests he has taken inspiration from that grisly metaphor. The scene begins *in medias res*, with Father Pirrone in attendance as well and the Prince railing at Sedàra because

The Prince pops the question ... and seals the deal

the mayor has somehow violated the protocols of the meeting. Whatever he did prompts the Prince to remind Sedàra that the Prince is the one who has invited him. But the Prince calms down and produces the letter he has received from Tancredi expressing his love for Angelica, and – chewing on some bits of toad – asks the mayor for his daughter's hand on Tancredi's behalf. The mayor is silent for some time, claiming to be overcome with emotion, before explaining that he knows his daughter will be only too happy to accept the proposal, whereupon the Prince stands, strides around his desk, looms over an obviously frightened Sedàra, then physically lifts the man up and kisses him on both cheeks.

Donnafugata, Sedàra's town

The most unpleasant part of the toad repast comes next, as the Prince explains what Sedàra already knows – that a young man of Tancredi's delicacy and distinction could never have been formed 'without his ancestors having squandered a half-dozen fortunes'. Now it is Don Calogero's turn to speak. He details a dowry of such staggering dimensions – acres and acres of olive groves, vineyards and wheatfields, not to mention twenty linen sacks, each filled with 10,000 ounces of gold – that Father Pirrone clucks his tongue and then tries to duplicate the sound to disguise his astonishment. Even the Prince finds the amount staggering, as his expression shows, though he says nothing to betray his realisation that the mayor is far wealthier than he supposed. As Don Calogero continues to talk about the vast dowry, he walks up to a map of Donnafugata featuring the Salina family crest, whereupon the camera zooms in on the map until it fills the screen. The visual message is unmistakable: if this is not already Don Calogero's town, it soon will be.

'My family means everything to me,' Sedàra says, which cues an unusual flashback to the early morning mass when Don Ciccio caught a glimpse of the mayor's beautiful wife (played by Cardinale in a double role). The voiceover is identical to what we heard the gamekeeper say only a few minutes of screentime before, suggesting that we are not watching a flashback so much as the

Prince's imagined version of Don Ciccio's secret encounter. When the 'flashback' ends, the toad having been successfully swallowed, the scene concludes with more comic business: Don Calogero announces that his family is also noble, or soon will be, once all the papers are in order. He is still speaking as the Prince strides out of the room screen left and we hear a door slam. Sedàra turns to Father Pirrone to explain that his daughter is on the verge of becoming 'the Baronessina Sedàra del Biscotto'. The priest smiles and repeats the name 'Biscotto' before he, too, walks out of the room, screen right. Don Calogero is still speaking when we hear the slam of another door, leaving the man gesturing to himself in the empty room.

The next scene opens with the Prince entertaining his family by reading aloud from Giulio Carcano's *Angiola Maria* (1839), a sentimental novel about a poor country girl who falls in love with a wandering English nobleman who, after getting what he wants, leaves her to die of a broken heart. The published screenplay has the Prince reading from another novel, Niccolò Tommaseo's *Fede e bellezza* (Faith and beauty) (1852),[68] but Visconti reverts to the book named in the novel, perhaps because the passage that the Prince reads – 'the description of the heroine's journey through the icy Lombard winter' (p. 145) – includes material roughly analogous to the present action in the film: a journey by horse through a violent storm. Even as the

Family entertainment

Prince reads, Tancredi and his companions are approaching the palace, having ridden through a thunderstorm. The choice of novel is of a piece with the overall authenticity of the scene: *Angiola Maria* is at an appropriate moral and sentimental level for domestic consumption. The Prince's son Francesco Paolo and Father Pirrone listen attentively, while the women – the Princess, the daughters Concetta, Carolina and Caterina; and the French governess, Mademoiselle Dombreuil – busy themselves with their knitting and other handicrafts. The room itself, with its brocaded furniture, Turkish carpets, portraits and paintings, all gently lit by the fire and the two oil lamps, is the very picture of a nineteenth-century drawing room, opulent but tasteful.

The sense of the space is compounded when the servant Mimi hears something and rushes out of the room, opening a series of doors to show the remarkable expanse of the palace in deep focus. Mimi returns to announce the surprise arrival of Tancredi, at which news Concetta lets out an involuntary 'Cara!', a romantic epithet overtaken by amorous events, unseen but undeniable, since the last time the Prince's nephew was in Donnafugata. He enters the room, soaking wet, with his friend and fellow officer Carlo Cavriaghi, as well as his orderly. This is Cavriaghi's second visit to the Salina household, having come to Palermo earlier with Tancredi and the Garibaldian general. They are wearing different uniforms now: in another example of Visconti's scrupulous eye for detail, Tancredi's has silver buttons with an orange collar and leg stripes, whereas Cavriaghi's has gilt buttons and crimson trimmings (the historically accurate garb of officers in, respectively, the cavalry and the infantry).[69] The Prince is puzzled by the new uniforms: 'Shouldn't you Garibaldini be wearing a red shirt?' The two officers react to the name with disdain: when Garibaldi's army disbanded, they became officers in 'the *real* army': 'the regular army of His Majesty, King of Sardinia, … and shortly to be of Italy' (p. 149). The change of army is one example of how opportunistic Tancredi is, and the presence of Cavriaghi is another: he is there as a replacement for Tancredi in Concetta's affections. One purpose of Tancredi's visit is to present Angelica with an engagement ring (purchased with his uncle's money). He shows the ring to everyone in the family, including Concetta, who walks out of frame once she sees it. Cavriaghi goes to console Concetta, not with a ring, but with a book of poetry by the neoromantic Aleardo Aleardi, inscribed with the words *Sempre sorda* (Forever deaf) because, Cavriaghi explains, Concetta is 'deaf to my sighs'. At this point Angelica shows up, dripping wet from the rain, and Tancredi rushes to embrace her, takes the ring from the box, places it on Angelica's finger and kisses her hard on the mouth. The camera is so tight at this moment all the other characters seem to have been forgotten, though we know they are watching.

One kiss … leads to another

What follows is very close to a match cut (call it a kiss cut), with Angelica and Tancredi in another lip-lock, but the costume and set changes mean we are now at another time and place. The time can't be more than a few days since the last kiss and the place is easy enough to work out: it's still the Donnafugata palace, but one of many disused rooms that Tancredi and Angelica wander through in defiance of their would-be chaperone, Mademoiselle Dombreuil. The governess can be heard calling out for the two lovers, who keep running from room to room, playing hide-and-seek and kissing passionately when one finds the other. It all seems rather childish, which raises the question of the respective ages of the couple. Aside from the youthful appearance of the pair, the film itself provides no specific information on this point, but the novel says Angelica is seventeen in 1860 and Tancredi twenty-one (Cardinale turned twenty-four and Delon twenty-seven in 1962 when the film was shot). Cardinale adopts certain mannerisms, such as biting her lower lip and widening her eyes over the discovery of something previously unknown, to convey the immaturity of the character, whereas Delon's Tancredi, however young, is already a man of the world, a soldier wounded in battle, after all. As the couple chase each other through room after room, Angelica stumbles onto an old bedroom. Tancredi finds her and caresses her heaving breasts as the couple collapse together on the bed. But he restrains himself, refusing to 'take her' until she is his wife. The long scene ends when Cavriaghi finds the couple and complains to Tancredi that Concetta will never love him. His friend says it's just as well – Concetta is too much of a Sicilian to adapt to his Milanese ways.

Meanwhile, another northerner arrives at Donnafugata: Chevalley di Monterzuolo, an emissary from the new government in Turin, has come to ask the Prince to accept an appointment as senator of Sicily. Chevalley is eager to conduct his business and leave the next morning, but the aggressive hospitality of the Prince dictates that he stay longer. That evening, the Prince partners with Chevalley in a game of whist, the card game of English origins favoured by cultivated Europeans in the nineteenth century, against Tancredi and Father Pirrone, while Cavriaghi keeps score. Chevalley is comforted by the presence of a fellow northerner when Francesco Paolo comes over and regales the ambassador with stories of Sicilian treachery, like the one about a family who could not pay the ransom on their kidnapped son and so received the boy back 'in instalments' – starting with an index finger and ending with the head, delivered in a basket, covered with fig leaves (in the novel, this story is told by Tancredi). Tancredi tells another gruesome story about a priest killed by poisoned communion wine, a civilised, Catholic form of murder, more 'liturgical' than, say, shooting. Chevalley is disturbed by the stories and insists that the new political order will put an end to such backwardness. The scene is comic, but it serves as a prelude to the next one, where Chevalley tries to persuade the Prince to join the new government and help to reform his homeland with progressive policies. In this, Chevalley is like Cavour – indeed, Leslie French has been made up to resemble the Italian Prime Minister – but the likeness is also a reminder that the new government sought to strongarm Sicilians into submission, evident when Chevalley first refers to the new nation as the result of 'the happy annexation' of the South by the North before he corrects himself: 'I mean, after the glorious union of Sicily and the Kingdom of Sardinia' (p. 173).

Chevalley

BENSO DI CAVOUR CONTE CAMILLO

Camillo Benso, Count of Cavour
(Lithograph, Ferdinando Perrin, 1867)
(courtesy Biblioteca di storia moderna e
contemporanea, Rome)

The interview with Chevalley takes place in the same room as the earlier talk with Sedàra about the marriage contract. That base conversation, in which negotiating with the mayor is likened to chewing on a toad, has this discussion as its more elevated counterpart, though both are really about the same thing: the place of the old ruling class in the new political order. In the earlier negotiations with Don Calogero, the Prince did what he had to do to align old values with new money. In the present colloquy with Chevalley, no such accommodation is possible: the old values and the new politics are simply incompatible. The dialogue in the scene follows the novel almost verbatim, as the Prince tries to make the diplomat understand the reasons for his refusal to accept the offer of a senatorial appointment, which boil down to the reactionary claim that progress is impossible for the Sicilian people, whose belief in their own 'perfection' makes them immune to improvement, having withstood centuries of invasions and colonisation by outsiders. Why should the new government be any different, the Prince asks, since, from the Sicilian perspective, it amounts to yet another imposition of authority by foreigners. The Prince also claims he lacks the essential quality of self-delusion necessary to ignore the age-old realities of his homeland, but he knows someone who likewise lacks illusions but can manufacture them if required: Don Calogero Sedàra. Chevalley has heard talk of

Sedàra and rejects the suggestion outright: such men, in possession of neither scruples nor vision, will make progress impossible, 'and then everything will be as before for more centuries' (p. 182). With that, the Prince announces that it is time for dinner and gives Chevalley permission to leave at dawn.

The chiming of the clock in Don Fabrizio's study serves as a sound bridge to the clanging of church bells, rousing Don Ciccio from an early morning nap in the village square: he is there with the hunting dogs for another shooting expedition with the Prince. This scene was shot in natural light, so the camera – and the microphone – both capture an actual dawn that includes two perfect fortuitous details: the sound of a rooster crowing at the start of the scene and a shot of a dog stretching to wake itself up at the end. When the Prince and Chevalley emerge from the palace, Don Ciccio follows them through a warren of narrow streets that look not so different from an Aci Trezza neighbourhood in *The Earth Trembles*. Chevalley pauses along the way to look at the sights of human squalor caused by centuries of poverty and shakes his head, no doubt thinking of the Prince's refusal to participate in the new government's plans for social improvements. Once they reach the carriage, the thoughts of the two characters in the novel are presented as dialogue. Chevalley says, 'This state of things won't last; our lively new modern administration

Peasants working to a waltz

will change it all,' and the Prince replies, 'All this shouldn't last; but it will.' Once Chevalley is in the carriage, the Prince continues, speaking almost to himself: 'We were the Leopards, the Lions; those who'll take our place will be little jackals, hyenas; and the whole lot of us, Leopards, jackals, and sheep, we'll all go on thinking ourselves the salt of the earth' (p. 185). At the end of this scene the camera pans to a group of peasants hoeing the fields, working to the tune of a waltz, another sound bridge to the 46-minute-long conclusion of the film.

The long exterior shot of the peasants dissolves to a long interior shot of an ornate ballroom, with men in tailcoats and women in ballgowns dancing a waltz. We are back in Palermo, at the estate of Don Diego Ponteleone and his wife, Donna Margherita. The date is November 1862, according to the novel; but all we know from the film is that the action is set sometime after 29 August 1862, the date of Garibaldi's wounding at Aspromonte, a mountain range in southern Calabria. Vittorio Emanuele II and his generals seemed to have been acting at cross purposes by allowing Garibaldi and his private army of Redshirt volunteers to embark from Catania on his stated mission to march on Rome, only to stop his advance once he reached Calabria. As strange as it sounds, the government may have fomented the Garibaldian action and then put it down in order to persuade Napoléon III that the Papal States could be better defended by the Italian Royal Army than by French forces.[70] In any event, French governance of the Papal States continued until Napoléon III's forces were defeated by Prussia in the Franco-Prussian War that began in 1870, whereupon the regular Italian army took control of Rome, completing unification and establishing the Eternal City as capital of the Kingdom. The 'hero' of Aspromonte was Colonel Emilio Pallavicino, who easily defeated the army of Redshirt irregulars because Garibaldi ordered his forces not to fire on their fellow Italians. Some shots were exchanged anyway, and Garibaldi was wounded in his right ankle and left thigh.[71] When Pallavicino arrives at the ball, he is introduced as 'the victor of Aspromonte'. This early mention of the famous incident will be elaborated in some detail towards the end of the long segment, providing a measure of structure to a somewhat formless exploration of what seems a last-gasp celebration of Sicilian nobility on the eve of its demise.

The ball scene does pose a problem for anyone looking to understand the overall structure of the film, since the attention devoted to material that in the novel runs to about twenty pages, roughly a twelfth of the whole, seems disproportionate. More than one critic has done the maths: the ball segment runs for 46 of the film's 185 minutes, comprising 178 of 725 shots, or about a quarter of the total running time. The comparison is sometimes made to Marcel Proust's *Le Côté de Guermantes* (*The Guermantes Way*, 1920): 525 pages cover two and a half years but 110 – a fifth of the novel – describe a dinner that lasts two or three hours.[72] The segment is like a film within the film, and, as such, it has its own structure that can be divided into four clear sections, not counting an introduction and a coda: the first waltz and other dances; Don Fabrizio in the library, joined by Tancredi and Angelica; the second waltz, in which the other dancers give way to Angelica and the Prince dancing alone; and the supper outdoors, featuring Don Fabrizio's conversation with Pallavicino. The introduction, logically enough, comprises the guests arriving, while the coda, which is also the end of the film, has Tancredi, Sedàra, Angelica and the Salina women leaving in a carriage, while Don Fabrizio walks back to his palace alone at dawn, pausing on the way to kneel on the street out of respect to someone receiving the Last Rites (action that, in the novel, occurs before the ball, not after).

The long segment begins with the Ponteleones welcoming their guests, including 'the Principessa di Lampedusa', a witty nod from Visconti to a fellow aristocrat since no such Princess appears in the novel (another guest is 'Gioacchino Lanza' – the name of Lampedusa's adopted son). But the two most important guests are Colonel Pallavicino and Angelica Sedàra. These two guests are implicitly connected when someone says of Pallavicino's action at Aspromonte, 'Those musket shots came at an opportune moment.' In other words, had not Pallavicino acted on his orders to fire on an army of Sicilians and put down a republican revolution from below, the monarchist revolution from above organised by the Lombards and the Piedmontese might have foundered and so made it harder for things to stay the same. And things must remain the same for the sort of society represented by the hosts and the guests at the ball to persist. Tancredi says, 'This will be Angelica's debut in society.' In the novel, the word *società* is placed in scare quotes, and so is *il mondo* (meaning the beau monde of high society), to convey a sense of how dubious and compromised the world of high society has become. Don Calogero Sedàra's presence is by itself a sign of how far fashionable society has fallen, but Tancredi does his best to stage-manage the man whose only purpose is the social necessity of accompanying his daughter in public. He has taken his future father-in-law to a good tailor to ensure that his formal dress will be up to standards, even though the man himself 'lacks *chic*', a sign of which is the civilian service medal Sedàra wears: the Order of the Crown of Italy. Tancredi snatches the medal and pockets it, explaining, 'Here you need better than that.' The Order of the Crown of Italy was not established until 1868 to commemorate the unification of 1861,[73] but Visconti's – and Lampedusa's – use of the anachronism serves to detail Sedàra's unfailing gift for gaucheness.

The highlight of the first major scene of the ball segment occurs when Tancredi and Angelica waltz together. Tellingly, they

Tancredi and Angelica waltzing (with everyone else)

Exhaustion sets in

are lost amid the crowd of other dancers; the camera does close
in on them at one point, but the sense of spectacle is nothing like
what is to come, when Angelica dances with the Prince. The Prince,
meanwhile, wanders about, wishing he had foregone the occasion,
though he knows that would have been impossible: he is following
the iron protocols of his class. A touching moment comes when Don
Fabrizio catches sight of himself in a mirror and sees that he looks as
exhausted as he feels. Shortly after this, he walks into a golden salon
full of young women, some seated on an enormous pouf in the
middle of the room, and remarks on them to an unnamed friend.

The golden salon full of 'monkeys'

In the novel, the Prince regards the 'mob of girls incredibly short, unsuitably dark, unbearably giggly' as the consequence of 'the frequent marriages between cousins due to sexual lethargy and territorial calculations'. He suddenly feels like a zookeeper amid a band of female monkeys, expecting 'at any moment to see them clamber up the chandeliers and hang there by their tails' (p. 222). By projecting his own sense of decadence onto those around him, the Prince invokes something like the theory of racial degeneration that Cesare Lombroso was just beginning to explore in the early 1860s, a theory later to become notorious when Lombroso's student Max Nordau published the international bestseller *Entartung* (*Degeneration*) in 1892.

As the Prince walks out of the room full of degenerate 'monkeys', we hear the orchestra tuning for the next dance – a mazurka – and Colonel Pallavicino asks Donna Margherita to be his partner. She demurs at first but takes the colonel's hand for what seems to be a more formalised, less energetic version of the folk dance that originated in Poland. Napoléon's Hussars danced the mazurka with village girls in the march across Europe, and Frédéric Chopin reacted to this appropriation (not to mention the conquest of Poland) by giving nationalistic expression to the mazurka rhythm in a series of compositions for piano.[74] However much these political developments may have informed the initial popularity of the dance, its aristocratic assimilation into nineteenth-century ball culture ultimately rendered moot any residual political meaning of the mazurka. The dance features a series of spins and sideways hops that makes the colonel's invitation to his elderly hostess seem a bit odd, but, fortunately, they do not dance alone for long before they are joined by all the other dancers, including Tancredi and Angelica, who are clearly enjoying themselves. Sedàra, not so much: he continues to be socially uncomfortable, not knowing how to behave, but a smug look occasionally crosses his face as if to suggest that he knows all the wealth on display will inevitably flow in his direction, thanks, in part, to his daughter's marrying into Sicilian nobility.

The next scene of the ball segment begins when the Prince retires from the ballroom to the library. Up to this point in the film, almost everything has been shot using deep focus, making even the most distant features of a landscape or a room clearly visible. Now, however, the background is out of focus, and even the foreground, as we see when the Prince reaches towards a candle to light a match for his cigar. The cinematographic change is a way of approximating the limited point of view of the novel: here the focus is exclusively on Lancaster's expressive face as the Prince, sitting on a leather sofa, suddenly notices a painting on the wall opposite him: 'a good copy of Greuze's *Death of the Just Man*' (p. 227).[75]

In fact, the melodramatic eighteenth-century painting by Jean-Baptiste Greuze that Lampedusa calls *Death of the Just Man* is better known as *The Father's Curse: The Son Punished* (1778). The work has as its companion the earlier painting titled *The Father's Curse: The Ungrateful Son* (1777). Together, the two paintings form a variation on the narrative of the Prodigal Son, which in the Bible concerns a son who leaves home with his inheritance and squanders it, but whose father not only welcomes him back but also celebrates his return – an allegory of Christian redemption. In Greuze's version, the son leaves home over his father's virulent objections not as a wastrel intent on indulging himself but as a soldier going

Just the death of a man

to war. The second painting – the one that draws Don Fabrizio's attention – depicts the son returning too late to see his father alive. The film focuses not on the son's return but on the representation of the father's death, which the Prince imagines will be not unlike his own, except that the sheets will be dirtier and the women beside his deathbed more modestly dressed.

Such are the Prince's thoughts in the novel, which in the film are spoken out loud after Tancredi and Angelica join him in the library. Tancredi tenderly comforts his uncle and gently chides him for thinking so soon of his own death. Lest anyone think the relative youth and vigour of Lancaster work against the Prince's mordant philosophising, we need to remember that in 1860 Italian life expectancy was only 30.[76] (In the novel, Don Fabrizio is forty-seven at the time of the ball in 1862, the same age that Giulio Fabrizio di Lampedusa, the historical model for Don Fabrizio di Salina, would have been in 1862; Lancaster turned forty-nine in 1962 when the film was shot.) But the painting suggests another meaning, given that Tancredi is more like a son to Don Fabrizio than his real sons. This 'son' has also gone off to war, but in a reversal of the Greuze narrative that seems more like the Bible story, upon his return his 'prodigality' is rewarded.

Angelica also seeks to comfort Don Fabrizio, but she has an ulterior motive: she wants the Prince to dance with her, and when he agrees to do so after an initial gallant refusal, Angelica casts a pouting look at Tancredi and says, 'You see, Tancredi, how good Uncle is? No nonsense about him, like you. You know, Prince, he didn't want me to ask you; he's jealous' (p. 229). This scene plays very differently on the screen than on the page. In the novel, Tancredi maintains his characteristic confidence and good humour, treating his alleged jealousy as a joke, but Delon acts genuinely uncomfortable, casting his eyes down in embarrassment at the prospect of his own uncle as a romantic rival. Indeed, there is an erotic charge between Lancaster and Cardinale, as she caresses his cheek and he takes her hand and passionately kisses the palm. She has made him feel young again,

he says, as the melancholy mood evoked by the Greuze painting of
the dying man dissipates. The three of them leave the library for
the dancefloor.

Although Lancaster is supposed to have had a knee injury, he
cuts a commanding figure as the Prince leading Angelica in the waltz,
a tune by Verdi that is heard here for the first time. Visconti's editor
Serandrei had stumbled across the score, written for piano, which
Rota then scored for full orchestra. The other guests recognise the
importance of the moment (it's Angelica's debut, after all) and stand
aside to watch the performance, including Tancredi, who looks a little
sheepish, still nursing his jealousy. Without question, the Prince and
his future niece-in-law dance far more impressively than Tancredi and
Angelica did, either in their first waltz together or in the mazurka.
More than two minutes pass before the waltz ends and the Prince
kisses his partner's hand. For a moment, it seems the guests are going

The Prince and Angelica waltz: production still

The Prince and Angelica waltz: publicity still

to burst into applause, but, as Lampedusa says, 'Fabrizio had too
leonine an air for anyone to risk such an impropriety' (p. 231).

Angelica asks the Prince to dine with her and Tancredi, but Don
Fabrizio declines, knowing that she is only asking out of politeness:
an old man would be out of place with the young lovers. Instead, he
mingles with the crowd of guests about the serving tables laden with
lobster and the like, but he declines such elegant fare. Instead, he
takes a small plate of dessert cakes and makes his way outside, but
not before a distressed look crosses his face when he hears Sedàra
and another nouveau riche bourgeois remarking on the value of the
candelabra and wondering how much the Ponteleones' land is worth.

Supper outside

Outside, the camera tracks for more than thirty seconds past the guests in all their finery before it stops to show a table in the middle distance where Colonel Pallavicino is seated, then cuts to a closer shot, then back to the Prince, who hears the colonel boasting about his exploits at Aspromonte and says to himself, 'What a bore that man is!' Too late: Pallavicino has seen the Prince and invites him to his table. The Prince takes a seat and the colonel continues to self-mythologise, telling the story of his gallant behaviour with the wounded general, adding that the musket shots he ordered actually benefited Garibaldi, 'freed him from that rabble'. While it is true that

The colonel congratulates himself

the troops Garibaldi assembled for his abortive march on Rome in 1862 were lower on the social scale than those he led in his attack on the Bourbon forces in 1860, the Prince has heard enough. 'Don't you think you went too far, with all that hand kissing and cap doffing?' Don Fabrizio says, flashing some real anger that takes the colonel aback. The Prince calms down and excuses himself.

The scene shifts back to the golden salon, no longer occupied by the band of 'monkeys'. Angelica is fixing her face as Concetta looks on. Tancredi has been searching for his fiancée after a conversation with Colonel Pallavicino that we do not hear, but he recounts it to the two women when he finds them: he agrees with the colonel that Italy needs 'law and order' and also approves of Pallavicino's plan to execute the 'fanatics who went with Garibaldi, this very dawn'. 'And rightly so,' he adds. Concetta is shocked that Tancredi would say such a thing and chides him for doing so before stalking off. Angelica is unperturbed by the attitude that led Visconti to claim that had Tancredi lived in the twentieth century, he would have become a Fascist.[77] As the two lovers kiss, a long line of dancers skips past the couple, who join them. The line snakes outside and weaves around through the supper tables before going back inside. The part of this scene evoking Aspromonte is an interpolation, not only to the novel, but also to the history, at least to some degree. While it is true that several of the Redshirts that Garibaldi commanded at Aspromonte were taken prisoner and summarily executed, the king later granted amnesty to most of them, whereas regular soldiers who had deserted the royal army to join the Redshirts were imprisoned for years.[78] The situation in the film, in which the 'fanatics' are brought back to Palermo to face a firing squad, hardly suggests summary execution.

Meanwhile, Don Fabrizio has gone to a room transformed into a makeshift toilet by the addition of 'a row of twenty vast vats, by that time nearly all brimful, some spilling over' (p. 237). Once again, he looks at himself in a mirror and sees reflected on his face a mixture of exhaustion and sadness: a close-up shows that he is weeping. This, too, is an interpolation, making Visconti's Don Fabrizio much

The Leopard weeps

more sentimental than Lampedusa's, but the moment makes sense: he weeps not so much because of his own imminent demise, but for the death of a class. That meaning carries over into the present action of the party ending, the guests departing, thanking their hosts for the beautiful evening. When Colonel Pallavicino bids farewell, he announces that he is going back to his barracks because 'our work for the night is not quite over' – a reference to the firing squad. This comment seems designed to complement Tancredi's remark to his uncle that he has spoken to one Finzoni, evidently a politician, because the Prince interprets it to mean that his nephew will be a candidate in the next election.

The Prince asks Tancredi to order the carriage and see his wife and daughters home, since he prefers to walk – to get some fresh air and look at the stars. As the Prince makes his way through the streets of Palermo, a priest with a ciborium following an acolyte ringing a bell crosses his path: they are on the way to administer the Last Rites at the deathbed of somebody in one of the houses along the way. The Prince stops and kneels out of respect, then looks up at the sky and, addressing Venus, asks that faithful star, 'When will you give me an appointment less ephemeral, far from all this, in your own region of perennial certitude?' The following shots explain why Visconti moved this scene from before the ball to after: it also serves to suggest a

Death in the morning

sacrament for the Redshirt 'rabble', who that very moment are being executed. A shot of a sleeping Sedàra inside the coach follows, but he is awakened by the sound of gunfire – the firing squad. A reverse shot shows a smug reaction from Tancredi, as we hear Sedàra's voice: 'A fine army,' he says. 'It means business. Just what was needed for Sicily. We can rest easy now.' Visconti cuts back to the Prince, still kneeling. Church bells chime as he rises and begins to walk slowly down a side street to the left of the screen. The end title 'Fine' looms towards the viewer as the Prince disappears into the darkness, but not before he draws the attention of a stray cat, that *gatto* surely being a nod to just how diminished *il gattopardo* has become.

5 The Reception

The premiere of *The Leopard* at the Barberini Cinema in Rome on 27 March 1963 was a major cinematic event, attended by the full galaxy of Italian movie stars, including Gina Lollobrigida, Monica Vitti, Vittorio Gassman, Marcello Mastroianni, and many others. The stars were there as nominees for the Nastri d'Argento (Silver Ribbon) awards at the annual ceremony for best achievements in Italian cinema put on by the SNGCI (Sindacato nazionale giornalisti cinematografici italiani/Union of Italian Film Journalists). The event was widely covered by the Italian press and television as a truly momentous and swank affair: newsreels show men in black tie and women in furs arriving at the Barberini, making their way through throngs of star-struck fans. Claudia Cardinale's escort for the evening was Visconti himself, but Burt Lancaster could not attend, reportedly 'sick with a virus'.[79] Only films released in 1962 were in competition, but the producer Goffredo Lombardo received a special award for the entirety of his oeuvre, not specifically for *The Leopard*. The excitement generated by the premiere carried over for weeks thereafter when the film went into limited distribution in Italy. *Variety* reported that by 14 April the film had taken in $370,000 (roughly $3.5/£2.8 million today) over ten days, setting box-office records at eight Italian venues and doing especially good business at theatres in Rome and Milan – the 'highest current average on the market', in fact.[80]

The first opportunity for international recognition came in May 1963 at the sixteenth edition of the Cannes Film Festival, where Visconti took home the Palme d'Or, the award for best overall picture. That year the festival opened with Alfred Hitchcock's *The Birds* (1963), screened out of competition; Federico Fellini's *8½* also premiered at the festival, likewise out of competition. Among the twenty-six films that competed for the Palme d'Or, notable entries included Robert Aldrich's *What Ever Happened to Baby Jane?* (1962), Robert Mulligan's *To Kill a Mockingbird* (1962), Lindsay Anderson's *This Sporting Life* (a 'kitchen sink' classic of the British New Wave, 1963), Ermanno Olmi's *I fidanzati* (*The Engagement*, 1963), Peter Brook's *Lord of the Flies* (1963) and Masaki Kobayashi's *Seppuku* (*Harakiri*, 1962) (which won a Special Jury Prize). These films aside, the twenty others in competition for the 1963 Palme d'Or have been largely forgotten. The relatively lacklustre competition is only one reason to qualify the cultural triumph of *The Leopard* at Cannes in 1963, given that the awards for screenplay and acting went to other films.

At the Silver Ribbon ceremony in April of the following year, Lombardo lost out to Angelo Rizzoli, who took the production prize for Fellini's *8½*. Fellini also won the Silver Ribbon for Best Director, considered the top award at the ceremony because no prize is given for best film. *8½* also won for Supporting Actress (Sandra Milo), Screenplay, Original Story, Black-and-white Cinematography and Score – the latter won by Nino Rota, whose score for *The Leopard* was not even nominated. All told, *8½* fairly swept the Silver Ribbons, winning seven of the thirteen categories for which it was eligible, compared to only three for *The Leopard*, all in technical or artistic categories: Colour Cinematography (Giuseppe Rotunno), Art Direction (Mario Garbuglia) and Costumes (Piero Tosi). In late July, at the David di Donatello Awards – the so-called 'Italian Oscars' geared more to commercial success than artistic quality – *The Leopard* won, or, rather, shared the award for Best Production, the co-winner being André Cayatte's *Le Glaive et la balance* (*Two Are Guilty*, 1962), a forgettable crime drama starring a French-speaking Anthony Perkins alongside Jean-Claude Brialy and Renato Salvatori. But Fellini bettered Visconti again at the Grolle d'oro (Golden Grail) festival, taking the top prize for directing (as with the Silver Ribbons, there is no award for best film). At the 1964 Étoile de cristal Awards (The Crystal Star, forerunner of the César Awards, the 'French

Oscars'), Burt Lancaster picked up the Best Foreign Actor prize for his performance in the French-dubbed *Le Guépard*.

Its middling performance on the European awards circuit notwithstanding, in Italy the phenomenal sales of Lampedusa's novel all but guaranteed an audience for a film based on it – provided the film was sufficiently faithful to the novel. For the most part, the popular press paid scant attention to Visconti's political interventions – the battle for Palermo and the execution of the Aspromonte 'traitors' – focusing instead on how carefully and thoroughly the director had evoked the vanished world imagined by the author. Giovanni Grazzini in *Corriere della Sera*, for instance, went so far as to suggest that Lampedusa himself would have delighted in the adaptation.[81] Grazzini was not alone among critics who imagined the author of the novel 'watching' the film from beyond the grave and approving of it. One critic claimed that 'if Giuseppe Tomasi di Lampedusa could see the film that Luchino Visconti made from his novel "The Leopard", he would not find anything substantially different from his own narration'. Pietro Bianchi, the film critic for *Il giorno*, likened *The Leopard* to *Gone with the Wind*, except that it was 'more brilliant, more authentic', and more accessible than Victor Fleming's film about the American Civil War. Bianchi added, 'Luchino Visconti remained substantially faithful to the novel. But above all, faithful to himself, taking the opportunity to pick up a dialogue that began from "Senso."'[82]

Even as the popular success of the novel ensured a like success with one type of audience for the film, for another type of audience the book became a kind of negative standard against which Visconti's Communist bona fides might be measured. As we have seen, leftist critics judged the novel harshly for a range of ideological reasons, most of which boil down to the double charge that Lampedusa combined nostalgia for the old regime with pessimism about the new one and did so in a retrograde, traditional literary form, making *The Leopard* a reactionary expression of bourgeois values. So, if the film was faithful to the novel, how could the political values expressed in cinematic form be all that different from those expressed in literary form? Had the northern aristocrat who adapted the novel compromised his Communist ideology by being true to the southern aristocrat who wrote the novel, widely judged as 'reactionary' by the left? Today, these kinds of questions seem simplistic in the extreme. At the very least, Lampedusa's account of the founding of Italy is ambiguous, but many of its omniscient, post-facto passages are richly ironic, as when the narrator reaches far into the future to hint at the craven nature of both Tancredi's and Sedàra's political careers: one may be an aristocrat and the other a bourgeois, but both are self-serving opportunists who hardly have the public welfare of the new nation-state as their primary objective. This omniscient dimension of the novel provides a measure of political critique that is missing from the film, so an argument could be made that Lampedusa allows for more ideological scepticism about the Risorgimento than Visconti. Be that as it may, after the film premiered in Italy several prominent Communist intellectuals registered their disapproval.

Visconti was well aware of the debates about the political and artistic merits of Lampedusa's novel, so his film could be understood as a partial commentary on those debates or even an active intervention into them. The choice to stage the Battle of Palermo, for example, is one such intervention, especially the scene where the group of citizens, many of them women, chase down the Bourbon collaborator and lynch him for his role in ordering the execution of their fellow citizens by firing squad. Leftist intellectuals associated with the PCI faulted Visconti for not including more such scenes, especially since the director was supposed to have had a more 'generous ideological commitment', as the film reviewer for the Communist newspaper *L'Unità* put it, to the social and political problems of the Mezzogiorno.[83] The Gramscian Marxist Guido Aristarco wrote in *Cinema nuovo* that Visconti had an 'acritical, immobile veneration' for the novel, which meant that the film was missing that 'breadth of historical vision' the critic had discerned in *Senso*.[84] The negative criticism of Visconti for being too faithful to the novel depends, of course, on the assumption that the novel was, in fact, a 'book of the right' and, as such, was as uniformly 'reactionary' as the left had depicted it.

Visconti must have anticipated these types of critiques in the Communist press because he appears to have orchestrated a counterresponse by going over the heads of the reviewers and appealing directly to the party leadership. He arranged a private screening for Palmiro Togliatti,[85] one of the founders of the PCI who had led the organisation for decades. Togliatti was impressed, judging the film 'a great work of art' that improved upon the novel, which he found 'too smoky'(by which he seems to have meant 'vague') and 'full of unfulfilled claims', a criticism that assumes that literature is in the business of making claims. Most importantly, Togliatti urged Visconti not to make any cuts, singling out the long ball segment in particular for its 'obsessive character', an odd but positive assessment that one finds only, he claimed, in the culmination of 'great artistic creations'.[86] These sentiments were expressed in a letter to Antonello Trombadori, a PCI deputy and a man of extraordinary culture who was one of Visconti's friends. As a Communist art critic, Trombadori had long sought to articulate the grounds on which the conflicting perspectives of art and politics might be reconciled, believing that the separation of art and life could be overcome; in fact, 'great art' consisted precisely of the reunion of the two.[87] This kind of thinking explains why Trombadori defended the film against Marxist charges of decadence, writing to Visconti with assurances that the director had been more faithful to the PCI than the PCI had been to him.[88] While the film was in production, Trombadori interviewed Visconti, their exchange subsequently appearing in the book edited by Suso Cecchi d'Amico published only days after the release of the film.

Trombadori begins the interview by laying out the basic terms of the Lampedusa 'case': whereas some critics fault the author for being a 'reactionary ... prisoner of an immobile vision of life', others credit him with writing 'the first modern Italian novel' to address 'the history and dramatic complexity of our national and spiritual formation. What is your position?' Visconti responds that he, too, shares Lampedusa's pessimism, though one not coloured with nostalgic regret over the collapse of the old feudal order ruled by the Bourbon kings, but with an active, wilful resolve to work towards a new social order. In addition to this positive pessimism, Visconti says he also shares the historical view of the Risorgimento as '"a failed revolution" or rather "betrayed"'. Moreover, he attributes this familiar Gramscian critique to Lampedusa himself, singling out 'the reflections of the prince during the outburst of Don Ciccio Tumeo on the results of the plebiscite' (i.e. the omniscient comment about 'the stupid annulment' of liberty (p. 113)).[89] Visconti's position, then, is quite shrewd: he defuses criticism of his film for its excessive fidelity to the novel by arguing that Lampedusa's attitude towards the Risorgimento is not dissimilar to Gramsci's, even though that attitude is regretful, not revolutionary. Visconti may not have completely insulated himself from leftist attacks by enlisting the support of such influential Communist leaders as Togliatti and Trombadori, but at least those attacks lost some of their force.

The American and British response to the film was extremely different from its reception in Italy and Europe more generally because the English-language version was not the film Visconti intended. At the 1964 Academy Awards, *The Leopard* received no awards at all. It was not even nominated in the Foreign Language Film category, the film's only nomination going to Tosi for Costume Design (Color) (won by the design team for *Cleopatra*, 1963). The underwhelming showing at the Academy Awards resulted in large part from the arrangements the production company Titanus was forced to make with 20th Century-Fox after another big-budget production, Robert Aldrich's *Sodoma e Gomorra* (*The Last Days of Sodom and Gomorrah*, 1962), brought the Italian company to the verge of bankruptcy. In exchange for a cash infusion of $2 million (close to $20 million in today's currency), Fox received the rights to US distribution. Two additional conditions of the deal were that the Prince be played by an American star and the film be made in English. In the end, Visconti settled on two different versions of the film, one in Italian, one in English, though he had no active role in the modifications to the Italian version that resulted in the film that Fox distributed. For the Italian version, Lancaster's contract with Fox stipulated that his scenes be shot in English, but the actor dropped that requirement,[90] allowing actors to perform on set in several languages (Cardinale, for example, spoke French in her scenes with Delon, English with Lancaster and Italian with most of the other actors). In post-production, all the voices were dubbed into Italian, including Cardinale's, whose voice was replaced by that of Solvejg D'Assunta (a minor actress but a major dubber).[91] For the American release, Lancaster and Leslie French, who played Chevalley, spoke their own lines, but the voices of the other characters were transformed into contemporary-sounding American English by actors mostly based in New York City, where the dubbing was done.[92]

Curiously, Visconti had ceded responsibility for the American release to Lancaster, who recommended that Fox executives ask his friend Sydney Pollack to cut the film down, do the sound mixing and manage the dubbing into English, which included supervising the post-synching of Lancaster himself. At this point in his career, the 29-year-old Pollack was a journeyman director of television series like *Wagon Train* (1957–65) and *Ben Casey* (1961–6), the feature films for which he is best known today (*The Way We Were* (1973), *Tootsie* (1982), etc.) lying far in the future.[93] Pollack later took the blame for butchering a masterpiece, acknowledging in an interview years later that it made no sense to dub the film because having the Italian characters speak English was entirely incongruous with Visconti's scrupulous attention to historical accuracy.[94] In fact, when he set out to rework *The Leopard* Pollack dismissed the importance of Italian history as something of interest only to Italians.[95] A good example of this attitude is the scene where the Prince goes to vote in the plebiscite and refers to Sedàra as 'the Cavour of Donnafugata': in the American version he says, 'the Napoléon of Donnafugata', which makes no sense at all.

A deleted scene: the Prince and a Parisian cocotte

But the dubbing was only one way in which the Fox version departed from the Titanus version. When the film had its official premiere at Cannes, it ran for 195 minutes, having been cut by Visconti from 205 minutes. He shortened the film by an additional 10 minutes for its theatrical release, so the 185-minute version may be regarded as the 'director's cut'. The 'archive' of some of the material he deleted survives in an Italian trailer, such as a strange scene at the inn on the journey to Donnafugata in which the Prince has a dream about a Parisian cocotte. Fox edited the film down still more and produced the version that runs for 161 minutes, 24 minutes under the director's preferred length. A number of scenes are shortened, often in ways that lead to confusion or, at least, reduce the significance of certain actions. For example, the Battle of Palermo shows the women chasing the Bourbon collaborator but omits his lynching, so the full meaning of that scene is constrained. Likewise, when the carriages bearing the Prince and his family on the way to Donnafugata arrive at the blockade, we hear Tancredi shout, 'The Prince of Salina! Open the barricades!' The carriages pass through without the exchanges between Tancredi and the soldiers, so the viewer of the 1963 Fox release could not have appreciated how assured and imperious Tancredi has become, nor would that viewer have fully understood the aristocratic privilege implicit in the scene.

The next scene is the luncheon on the grass, the overnight stay at the rustic inn having been cut entirely, so the audience of the American version missed Father Pirrone's detailed speech to the peasants about the progress of the revolution and his explanation of how different the aristocracy is from everyone else, not to mention the beauty of the cinematography evocative of Caravaggio's painting.

Once the scene shifts to Donnafugata, major cuts are made to the exchanges between Don Ciccio and Prince Fabrizio on their hunting trip: we never hear how Sedàra has accumulated his wealth, nor do we hear about his beautiful but illiterate wife, the daughter of the disgusting peasant, Peppe 'Mmerda. This omission necessitates another one: the fantasy scene of Don Ciccio at early mass catching a glimpse of Angelica's beautiful mother. The scene of Chevalley trying to convince Prince Fabrizio to accept the invitation to represent Sicily in the senate of the new government is presented in full, but the earlier scene where Paolo Francesco and Tancredi regale Chevalley with tales of Sicilian treachery is omitted. The ball scene is mostly intact, reduced by about four minutes from the 46 minutes of the Italian version, but some cuts occur at key moments, such as the brief but remarkable series of facial expressions Stoppa uses to signify Sedàra's smug sense of how well he will fare in the new social order.

The Fox brain-trust also reduced the film from its original 70mm Super Technirama format shot in Eastmancolor processed by Technicolor to 35mm CinemaScope processed by De Luxe (both CinemaScope and De Luxe were Fox subsidiaries).[96] Technirama was a fairly new technology, the first film branded as such being Samuel A. Taylor's *Montecarlo* (1956), an Italian comedy-drama released for the English-speaking market as *The Monte Carlo Story*, produced by Marcello Girosi, an executive with Lombardo's company Titanus. In the trade magazine *Motion Picture Daily*, Girosi touted the advantages of 'the new process, which employs film traveling horizontally through the camera, as "two-fold in its benefits"', the first being '"the wonderful detail, the superb focus, which catches natural beauties and details as much as a thousand feet away"'.[97]

That advantage is one of the most striking features of *The Leopard*, with the details of distant landscapes appearing as sharp and clear as objects in the foreground. The second advantage, Girosi said, '"was the process of printing in any format required, such as CinemaScope, VistaVision, regular 35mm, etc."'.[98] This second alleged benefit proved to be a liability that all but negated the advantages of the first one Girosi described. When Visconti saw the CinemaScope/De Luxe version Fox distributed, he disowned the film in an open letter published in *The Times* and other newspapers, complaining that it had been 'deeply transformed in regard to the original one, through the cuts and, to an even higher degree, through the modification of the printing system, which caused a complete alteration of

Luncheon on the grass: Titanus version; Fox version

the colour'.[99] Fox vice president Seymour Poe threatened to take legal action against Visconti, claiming that the director 'seems dedicated to harming his own picture with a series of negative statements which seem to denigrate the film'.[100]

Visconti's comment about colour alteration is evident in the contrast of the vivid hues of the original and the pastel palette of the Fox version. But the most striking difference between the two versions lies in the resolution of the image, which is much sharper in the original Titanus version. The 70mm Super Technirama format is non-anamorphic, unlike regular Technirama and other widescreen formats of the time, such as VistaVision, Todd-AO and CinemaScope. These anamorphic formats were produced by adding a special attachment to the camera that squeezed or distorted the image so it would fit onto a 35mm frame during filming (as with *The Monte Carlo Story*). Films made using this technology also employed a special projector attachment for exhibition that 'unsqueezed' or widened the image when projected.[101] To oversimplify, what came out of the projector in the case of films shot using the non-anamorphic 70mm Super Technirama process was much closer to what went into the camera in the first place. In the case of the Italian version, what went onto the 70mm frame was meant to come out as an image with a 2.21:1 aspect ratio (meaning that the width of the image is roughly two and one-fifth more than its height), but the American version that came out of the projector had first been squeezed onto 35mm film, then widened for exhibition to produce an image with a 2.35:1 aspect ratio (the width being about two and one-thirds greater than the height). That slight increase in the size of the image may be one reason the American *Leopard* is not as sharp as the Italian version, but the main reason, according to publicity materials promoting the rerelease of the film in 1983 as 'A 20th Century-Fox International Classic', was 'the use of a dupe negative with loss of color fidelity and definition' for the conversion.[102]

The difference between the original Titanus version and the first Fox release is well captured by Richard Roud, film reviewer for the *Guardian*. Roud was in a good position to make comparisons, having seen the version that premiered at Cannes:

Just how extraordinary Visconti's visual imagery was, no one who sees the present version will ever know. Visconti, who spends hours and days fretting over the colour of every little detail ... has had his film snatched from his hands. Screen shape has been altered and, even worse, colour system has been changed. The result is rather like those nice coloured postcards you can buy at the National Gallery. All the sharpness of definition has gone, a kind of veil creeps insidiously over the image, and of course the colours have changed colour. There are films where this wouldn't matter so much, but 'The Leopard' depends on sheer visual beauty for its very meaning.[103]

Roud also commented on the dubbing, making the somewhat snarky point that 'Burt Lancaster dubbed into Italian (as in the original version) *was* the Prince of Salina. Burt Lancaster using his own voice is just Burt Lancaster dressed up in fancy clothes.'[104]

Another factor that affected the American reception of Visconti's film was the way the Fox publicity machine marketed it. *The Leopard* was advertised as a film from the same studio that had produced *The Longest Day* (1962) and *Cleopatra*, both big-budget, star-studded efforts to counter the exodus of viewers from the movie theatre to the televisions in their living rooms. Fox also used Lancaster's star power to promote the film, reminding prospective viewers of his Best Actor Oscar for *Elmer Gantry*. The movie poster for *The Leopard* has his name above the title of the film and in the same sized font. Lancaster appears at the outset of one of the trailers for the film and dutifully repeats the studio line that 20th Century-Fox 'also gave you *The Longest Day* and *Cleopatra*'. Like most leading men of his era, Lancaster had several Westerns to his credit at the time (*Vengeance Valley* (1951), *Vera Cruz* (1954), *The Kentuckian* (1955), *Gunfight at the O.K. Corral* (1956) and *The Unforgiven* (1960)), which perhaps explains why the American trailer makes *The Leopard* look like another one: shots include the 'wagon train'

The poster for the Fox release (courtesy Margaret Herrick Library)

to Donnafugata, the Prince in a 'cowboy hat' with Don Ciccio firing rifles on the hunting trip, and the 'shootout' in Palermo. When an announcer takes over from Lancaster, the voice proclaims, '"A stunning visualization. Nostalgia very similar to *Gone with the Wind*," says Bosley Crowther of the *New York Times*.' This assertion is followed by shots of the red-shirted rebels in their grey trousers battling the Bourbons in their blue uniforms.

Fair enough: the Risorgimento in Italy does bear comparison with the Civil War in the US, but the announcer misrepresents Crowther, for whom the comparison is occasion to raise doubts about whether the film will play with American audiences: 'I just wonder how much Americans will know or care about what's going on, how much we will yield to a nostalgia very similar to that in "Gone With the Wind."' Crowther's overall review was mostly positive, but mixed; he found the film a 'remarkably vivid, panoramic and eventually morbid show', singling out for censure the dubbing that also irked the critic Roud: '[U]nfortunately Mr. Lancaster does have that blunt American voice that lacks the least suggestion of being Sicilian in the English-dialogue version shown here.' Of Delon, Crowther observes that he is 'handsome and physically correct as the Prince's high-spirited nephew, but ... the American voice that speaks for him is not appropriate'.[105] The critic followed up his initial review with some additional comments a few days later in which he praised the artfulness of the film but bewailed the lack of action: 'As much as one may be moved by the exquisite juxtapositions of characters and scenery, the itch of indifference and ennui may set one wriggling. It's action one wants.'[106]

Crowther's judgement about the pace of the film was echoed by other reviewers throughout the country. The *San Francisco Examiner* headlined its review 'The "Leopard" Beautiful, but Static',[107] the *Omaha World-Herald* said 'things seem to drag uncomfortably when ... the Lancaster image is not on the screen',[108] and the *Johnson City Press-Chronicle* asked, 'Does a movie have a right to bore its audience?'[109] The review headline in the *News* of Van Nuys, California, 'Toothless "Leopard," Set Loose, Meets With Total Indifference', turns out to have been more sensational than truthful, because the majority of reviews in the US were mostly positive. But even the positive reviews often came with the qualification that the appeal of the film was limited to certain types of audiences: '"The Leopard's" popularity will have to rest with admirers of the novel and the so-called class audience.'[110]

Both the marketing of *The Leopard* and the reviews in the American press are easy to read today as evidence of radical shifts in the film industry. The year 1963 is now understood as a watershed in the near-total collapse of the Hollywood studio system and, to a lesser extent, of the European studio system as well. *The Leopard* did not play as important a role as the disastrous *Cleopatra* in the problems 20th Century-Fox created for itself in 1963, but it did play a role. Moreover, Visconti's film has the dubious distinction of hastening the collapse of not one but two legendary production companies (although the unravelling of Lombardo's Titanus had begun the year before with *Sodom and Gomorrah*). Still, *The Leopard* did reasonably well with European audiences, just as it found a modicum of success in the US, but in neither case could box-office receipts offset the enormous cost of production (Lombardo reported the cost of the film as 2,900 million lira, i.e. 2.9 billion: more than £1.6 million in 1962, around £28 million in today's currency).[111]

The Leopard is, in many ways, the apotheosis of traditional film-making, involving high production values, big-name stars, a bestselling novel as the basis for the script, and, of course, a celebrity director. But it appeared before the public at a time when the elements of traditional film-making were coming into question. Indeed, Fellini's *8½* achieved critical acclaim (and commercial success) partly because it raised doubts about the very nature of traditional film-making. That said, the reception of *The Leopard* was no prediction of its legacy. Critics and audiences may have delighted more in Fellini's absurdist send-up of the movies in 1963, but in the years to come ever fewer films would look and feel like *8½*, while more and more would come to resemble *The Leopard*.

The reason for this tendency lies in the relationship of the two films to the cinematic context of the early 1960s, a period of enormous transformations in both the industry itself and the artistic choices of individual directors. Fellini's *8½* harmonises with such developments as the French New Wave and might be understood as an entry in the Italian New Wave if such existed (thanks to the continuing heritage of neorealism in Italy in the 1960s, the notion of a *nuova ondata* did not really take hold).[112] *8½* tells the visually fractured and narratively fractious story of the auteur director Guido Anselmi (Marcello Mastroianni) and his struggle to make a film when he claims he has 'nothing to say'. The film we watch has a lot in common with the film that the fictional auteur imagines, including flashbacks to childhood experiences and romantic entanglements involving his wife, his mistress and the beautiful woman (played by Claudia Cardinale) who stars in the film-within-the-film (and, obviously, in *8½*). All of this ambiguity and indeterminacy is represented by means of various meta-cinematic devices, as when the non-diegetic score becomes diegetic with Guido whistling a tune from the soundtrack the audience has just heard. Or when the fictional auteur appears in a shot that starts out from his own point of view.[113] This sort of self-conscious experimentation is nowhere to be found in *The Leopard*, the paradoxical result of which –

in terms of a broader history of cinematic tastes – is that a film like
8½ belongs more to its own time than does *The Leopard*, which
means that the impact of Fellini's film was more immediate, whereas
that of *The Leopard* has been more lasting. However much 8½
continues to be venerated by cinephiles, its avant-gardism now seems
a bit belated: today, it is much easier to imagine a contemporary
Leopard than a contemporary 8½.

But it would still take some time for Visconti's film to find its
legacy. *The Leopard* was part of the story of the early 1960s that saw
movie audiences gravitating away from big-budget fiascos like the
notorious *Cleopatra*. But the near-collapse of the old studio system
had the beneficial effect of opening up the cultural field to a new
generation of directors.[114] For a while, the success of independent film-
making made it seem that films like *The Leopard* would continue to
recede in cinema history, relegated to a bygone era of blockbusters and
superspectacular productions. But the major studios, now transformed
into media conglomerates, adapted to the new environment and
figured out a way to cash in on the fresh independent talent, a
signal example being Francis Ford Coppola, who started his career
assisting on cheap sexploitation films before directing his first feature,
Dementia 13 (1963), an independent horror flick produced by Roger
Corman. Coppola and other directors whom we now understand in
historical terms as part of the New Hollywood had either gone to film
school or schooled themselves in cinema history, so when Paramount
tapped Coppola to direct *The Godfather* (1972), that history was
activated as an important dimension of the film. The most obvious
homage to Visconti in *The Godfather* is the long wedding segment
that opens the film; though not as long (a mere 25 minutes or so),
it is comparable to the ballroom section of *The Leopard* in the lush
mise en scène and attention to period detail (albeit a very different
period). Also, the patriarch of the crime family, Don Corleone (Marlon
Brando), is similar to Don Fabrizio in that both are sensitive to their
own diminishing power and recognise the need for change so that
things can remain the same. In this respect, the modernising impulse

The wedding waltz in *The Godfather* (1972)

of the Godfather's son Michael (Al Pacino) is not unlike Tancredi's shrewd revision and renewal of aristocratic privilege.[115]

Visconti's influence on New Hollywood is even more apparent in the career of Coppola's fellow star director, Martin Scorsese. A film-maker thoroughly versed in cinema history, Scorsese brought his appreciation of Italian neorealism to his first feature, the crime drama *Mean Streets* (1973), not to mention the gritty character study *Taxi Driver* (1976). *Raging Bull* (1980), the biopic of the middleweight champion Jake La Motta, owes a lot to Visconti's importation of melodrama from the opera house to the boxing ring in *Rocco and His Brothers*. Regarding *The Leopard*, Scorsese has made several public comments about the importance of that film to his career. As founder and chair of The Film Foundation, he oversaw the 4K restoration of the film, which screened at Cannes in 2010. On that occasion, Scorsese introduced the film by remarking, 'I live with this movie every day of my life.'[116]

When asked by the Criterion Collection in 2014 to name his top ten films, he included *The Leopard*, saying, 'It's a film that has become more and more important to me as the years have gone by.'[117]

Scorsese's *The Age of Innocence* (1993): virtuoso shotmaking

The one film in Scorsese's oeuvre most clearly indebted to *The Leopard* is *The Age of Innocence* (1993), based on the Edith Wharton novel about high society in old New York published in 1920. Scorsese has acknowledged the influence of *The Leopard* (and *Senso*) on what he reluctantly calls his 'costume drama'.[118] The film is set in the 1870s, roughly the same period that Visconti recreates, and Scorsese, like Visconti, goes to great pains to convey an authentic sense of the times through a scrupulously detailed *mise en scène* composed of luxurious settings and lavish costumes. Granted, Scorsese's virtuoso shotmaking sometimes distracts from the period authenticity and his scenario is less concerned with political developments than Visconti's, but both films convey an acute understanding of social distinctions in their respective historical contexts.

In his lukewarm review of *The Age of Innocence*, the *New York Times* film critic Vincent Canby said that the static screenplay might have benefited from the talents of Ruth Prawer Jhabvala,[119] the scenarist for the films of Ismail Merchant and James Ivory, including *A Room with a View* (1985), *Howards End* (1992) and others in the genre now known as 'the heritage film'. The term emerged in the 1980s to describe (mostly) British films identifiable by high production values, scenarios adapted from classic novels, the cultivation of a 'touristic' gaze and, most importantly, the combination of national culture and conservative ideology.[120] At first, *The Leopard* seems hard to reconcile with this tendency because Visconti's Marxist politics involve more of a critical than a celebratory posture on Italian history. But the passage of time has rendered the ideological edge of the film, always problematic to begin with, less and less sharp. It may not have been a heritage film in 1963, but it might well be one now. The original Italian-language version was rereleased in 1983, just as the heritage film genre was taking hold, so it is understandable that audiences at that time would see it as another entry in the genre. Hence, there seems to be no doubt that the association of Visconti's film with the heritage genre is part of its reception, but is it part of its legacy?

The question goes to the heart of the characteristic tension in Visconti's career between his aesthetics and his politics, between his affection for decadence and his commitment to progress, between his aristocratic lineage and his Marxist sympathies, and so on. Here, the tension derives from the difference between one kind of historical representation and another, between a critical examination of national heritage and commercial exploitation of it. Since Visconti had a major role in driving one major studio (Titanus) to the verge of bankruptcy and a minor role in the collapse of another (Fox), it is hard to think of him as someone for whom historical vision was compromised by commercial concerns. In fact, it is easier to think of that vision as compromised not by commercial but by artistic concerns. After all, that is what his oft-critiqued abandonment of neorealism allegedly entails. Neorealism had been the preferred cinematic form of Italian national expression in the post-war period largely because it allowed the camera to capture reality in something close to an unmediated fashion – location shooting, natural light, non-professional actors, and the like. André Bazin's critique of Visconti included the charge that his brand of cinematic realism was too constructed, mediated overmuch by other arts, such as literature, painting, opera and so on – not immediate, like Rossellini's. For Bazin, even *The Earth Trembles* betrayed 'a dangerous inclination to aestheticism'.[121]

As awareness of the political conditions that so charged the reception of *The Leopard* in the 1960s continues to recede, its aesthetic appeal makes it look more and more like a 'heritage film'. The comparison is made easier by the proliferation today of big-budget, prestige productions like Peter Morgan's *The Crown* (2016–), Julian Fellowes's *The Gilded Age* (2022–) and perhaps even the second season of Mike White's *The White Lotus* (2022), filmed at different locations in Sicily, including Palermo. The latter explores the excesses of super-wealthy American tourists who indulge in vices ranging from adultery to murder at an absurdly upscale resort, its over-the-top depravity making it different from Morgan's more restrained but still sensational send-up of the aristocratic misadventures of the British royal family or Fellowes's tempered narrative of wasteful wealth and social ambition in belle époque New York. What they all have in common are the high production values and the cultivation of the voyeuristic 'tourist gaze' of heritage cinema, qualities that *The Leopard* shares. But, at the same time, these latter-day, big-budget productions remain, after all, small-screen, devised for streaming on a television or even a smartphone – a far cry from Super Technirama, to say the least. One of the best capsule definitions of decadence is 'decline at its peak', and while Luchino Visconti's *The Leopard* will always occupy a privileged place at the heights of all the aesthetic refinement and social corruption the best decadence entails, part of its legacy includes that lesser decadence so prominent in our own declining times.

Notes

1 Giuseppe di Lampedusa, *The Leopard*, trans. Archibald Colquhoun (New York: Pantheon, 2007), p. 28. Further references to this translation are cited parenthetically.

2 Giuseppe Tomasi di Lampedusa, *Il gattopardo*, 99th edn (Milan: Feltrinelli, 2013), p. 50. Suso Cecchi d'Amico (ed.), *Il film 'Il gattopardo' e la regia di Luchino Visconti* (Bologna: Cappelli, 1963), p. 44.

3 See Joan Ramon Resina, *Luchino Visconti: Filmmaker and Philosopher* (London: Bloomsbury, 2022), for a fuller discussion of Visconti and decadence. The focus of the book is on *La caduta degli dei* (*The Damned*, 1969), *Morte a Venezia* (*Death in Venice*, 1971) and *Ludwig* (1972), with *The Leopard* mentioned only in passing.

4 Written in 1926, Gramsci's essay 'Alcuni temi della questione meridionale' (Some themes regarding the Southern Question) was first published by the journal *Lo stato operaio*, but Gramsci had explored the question in an earlier essay, 'Operai e contadini' (Workers and peasants), published in the 3 January 1920 issue of *L'ordine nuovo*, the newspaper Gramsci founded. See Pasquale Verdicchio, introduction to Antonio Gramsci, *The Southern Question* (New York: Bordighera Press, 2015), pp. 1–2.

5 Antonio Gramsci, *Selections from the Prison Notebooks*, ed. and trans. Quintin Hoare and Geoffrey Nowell-Smith (New York: International Publishers, 1971), pp. 59, 70–1.

6 Ibid., p. 58. Gramsci did not coin the term *trasformismo*, which had been around since the 1880s and was used to describe 'the process whereby the so-called "historic" Left and Right parties which emerged from the Risorgimento tended to converge in terms of programme during the years which followed' (58*n*8).

7 Quoted in Denis Mack Smith, *The Making of Italy: 1796–1866* (London: Macmillan, 1968), p. 379.

8 Archibald Colquhoun, 'On Safari with Visconti', *Films and Filming* 9, no. 1 (October 1962): 11.

9 Curiously, even as Visconti was working on *The Leopard*, his brother Nicolo of the Carlo Erba pharmaceutical firm was indicted in October 1962 by a federal grand jury in New York for stealing formulas from a drug company in the US and manufacturing drugs in Italy without a licence to do so. See Edward Ranzal, '8 Held in Theft of Wonder Drugs', *New York Times*, 30 October 1962, p. 72.

10 David Gilmour, *The Last Leopard: A Life of Giuseppe Tomasi di Lampedusa* (London: Eland, 2007), p. 208.

11 Louis Aragon, 'Un grand Fauve se lève sur la littérature: *Le Guépard*', *Les Lettres françaises*, no. 803 (17–23 December 1959): 1, 5; Louis Aragon, 'Le Guépard et La Chartreuse', *Les Lettres françaises*, no. 812 (18–24 February 1960): 1–2.

12 Luchino Visconti, 'Io, Luchino Visconti, confessioni e ricordi raccolti da Aurelio Di Sovico', *Il mondo*, 8 January 1976, p. 69.

13 Luchino Visconti, 'Racconto storie come se raccontassi un requiem', in Adelio Ferrero, *Visconti: il cinema* (Modena: Stampa Cooptip, 1977), p. 81.

14 Guido Aristarco, 'Luchino Visconti: Critic or Poet of Decadence', trans. Luciana Bohne, *Film Criticism* 12, no. 3 (Spring 1988): 58–63.

15 Colquhoun, 'On Safari with Visconti': 10.

16 Dante Alighieri, *The Divine Comedy: Purgatorio*, Volume 2, ed. and trans. Robert M. Durling (Oxford: Oxford University Press, 2003), p. 128.

17 Geoffrey Chaucer, *The Canterbury Tales*, ed. Robert Boenig and Andrew Taylor, 2nd edn (Peterborough, ON: Broadview Press, 2012), p. 344. A modern English translation of these lines is: 'Great Bernabo Visconti of Milan, / God of indulgence, scourge of Lombardy.' See Geoffrey Chaucer, *The Canterbury Tales*, trans. Nevill Coghill (London: Penguin, 2003), p. 201.

18 Gaia Servadio, *Luchino Visconti: A Biography* (New York: Franklin Watts, 1983), pp. 6, 8.

19 These numbers do not include the operas that Visconti directed more than once, nor do they include the anthology films to which he contributed an episode. All told, Visconti directed twenty opera productions and directed twenty films, including the anthology films and several shorts. See Henry Bacon, *Visconti: Explorations of Beauty and Decay* (Cambridge: Cambridge University Press, 1998), pp. 247–59, 266–9.

20 See, for example, Ronald Bergen, *Jean Renoir: Projections of Paradise* (New York: Arcade, 2016), p. 140, who says Visconti 'was a lowly 27-year-old assistant on *Toni*'; and Bert Cadullo, *Screening the Stage: Studies in Cinedramatic Art* (Bern: Peter Lang, 2006), p. 68, who claims that Visconti 'had worked as Renoir's assistant on *Toni* … and several other films'.

21 Giuliana Minghelli, 'Neorealism', in Joseph Luzzi (ed.), *Italian Cinema:*

From the Silent Screen to the Digital Image (New York: Bloomsbury, 2020), p. 62.

22 Italo Calvino, 'Preface', *The Path to the Spiders' Nests*, trans. Martin McLaughlin and Archibald Colquhoun (New York: HarperCollins, 2000), p. 7.

23 In a 1959 interview, Visconti described how he worked on *The Earth Trembles* without a script by providing his subjects with a basic summary of the dramatic action. See Jean Domarchi and Jacques Doniol-Valcroze, 'Visconti Interviewed', *Sight and Sound* 28, nos. 3–4 (Summer–Autumn 1959): 144–7, 191.

24 Brendan Hennessey, '*Senso*', in Luzzi, *Italian Cinema*, p. 317.

25 As Louis Bayman observes in *The Operatic and the Everyday in Postwar Italian Film Melodrama* (Edinburgh: Edinburgh University Press, 2014), p. 173, Visconti puts melodrama to historical purpose, the 'operatics' of *Senso* being 'part of a national condition, a refusal of critical and progressive engagement in life for the indulgent pleasures of emotional fantasy'.

26 Roy Palmer Domenico, *Remaking Italy in the Twentieth Century* (Langham, MD: Rowman & Littlefield, 2002), p. 107.

27 Suso Cecchi d'Amico, Visconti's collaborator on the script, denied any intention to make *Senso* an implicit commentary on wartime and post-war Italy, but that position could have been part of an effort to prevent the censorship that, unfortunately, occurred. See Bacon, *Visconti*, pp. 70–1.

28 Geoffrey Nowell-Smith develops this contrast in some detail in *Luchino Visconti*, 3rd edn (London: BFI, 2003), p. 98.

29 Sam Rohdie discusses this topic in *Rocco and His Brothers* (*Rocco e i suoi fratelli*) (1992; London: BFI/Bloomsbury, 2020), p. 20.

30 This is the same region Carlo Levi described in *Cristo si è fermato a Eboli* (1945), his memoir of internal exile during the Fascist era. The book was made into a feature film by Francesco Rosi in 1979 and later released in expanded form as a television series.

31 Christopher Hibbert, *Garibaldi: Hero of Italian Unification* (New York: Palgrave Macmillan, 2008), p. 22.

32 Tommaso M. Cima, 'La realizzazione', in Cecchi d'Amico (ed.), *Il film 'Il gattopardo'*, p. 163. Unless otherwise indicated, details about the production are taken from this essay.

33 Caterina d'Amico de Carvalho, *Life and Work of Luchino Visconti* (Rome: Cinecittà International, [1997?]), p. 126.

34 Laurent Metzger, 'Relations between Marseille and East and Southeast Asia', in Arndt Graf and Chua Beng Huat (eds), *Port Cities in Asia and Europe* (Abingdon: Routledge, 2009), p. 24.

35 David Forgacs and Rossana Capitano, DVD commentary, *The Leopard* (*Il gattopardo*), dir. Luchino Visconti (London: BFI, 2004), DVD.

36 d'Amico de Carvalho, *Life and Work of Luchino Visconti*, p. 126.

37 The Villa Boscogrande is today an upmarket venue for weddings and corporate events, but the fake ceiling frescoes have survived (they are prominent on the Boscogrande's Instagram account and website), albeit altered to eliminate the heraldic figure of the serval rampant on the Lampedusa coat of arms.

38 Giuseppe Tomasi di Lampedusa to Baron Enrico di Tagliavia, 30 May 1957, in Gioacchino Lanza Tomasi, foreword, trans. Guido Waldman, to *The Leopard*, trans. Archibald Colquhoun, p. xii.

39 Costanzo Costantini, 'Luchino Visconti non potrà girare "Il Gattopardo" a Palma di Montechiaro', *Il Messaggero*, 4 May 1962, n.p. Jack Piler, 'Mafia Threats Keep Movie Men Moving', *Daily Herald*, 7 August 1962, p. 3.

40 Giuseppe Tomasi di Lampedusa, *The Siren and Selected Writings* (London: Harvill Press, 1995), p. 29.

41 Production Information Guide, p. 15, *The Leopard* clipping file, Billy Rose Theatre Collection, New York Public Library at Lincoln Center.

42 'Basta Pasta!', *Pittsburgh Post-Gazette*, 1 December 1962, p. 10.

43 d'Amico de Carvalho, *Life and Work of Luchino Visconti*, p. 126.

44 Claudia Cardinale, interview, *The Leopard* (*Il gattopardo*), DVD.

45 The first wife of Gioacchino Lanza Tomasi, Lampedusa's adopted son, is a guest at the ball, as well as her sister, who is among the group of young women sitting on the enormous pouf in the golden salon. The first Signora Tomasi was named Mirella – also the name of the character she plays. Nicoletta Pola Lanza Tomasi, email communication, 6 May 2023.

46 Cardinale, interview, *The Leopard* (*Il gattopardo*), DVD.

47 d'Amico de Carvalho, *Life and Work of Luchino Visconti*, p. 112.

48 Peter Bondanella and Federico Pacchioni, *A History of Italian Cinema*, 2nd edn (London: Bloomsbury, 2017), p. 426.

49 Kate Buford, *Burt Lancaster: An American Life* (Cambridge, MA: Da Capo Press, 2001), p. 222.

50 George Waldo, 'Burt Lancaster: Circus Acrobat Changes Spots for "Leopard"', *Los Angeles Times*, 21 October 1962, Calendar Section, p. 7.

51 Buford, *Burt Lancaster*, p. 225.

52 Waldo, 'Burt Lancaster', p. 7.

53 'Film Realism Is the Key', *The Spokesman-Review* (Spokane, WA), 1 July 1962, Family Section, part 2, p. 14.

54 On the one hand, there are reports that Visconti considered Stanislavsky his 'imaginative master'; on the other hand, Visconti sought to break free from the Stanislavsky tradition in his own production of *The Cherry Orchard*. See Buford, *Burt Lancaster*, p. 225, and Laurence Schifano, *Luchino Visconti: The Flames of Passion*, trans. William S. Byron (London: Collins, 1990), p. 353.

55 James Naremore, 'Acting in Cinema', in Pam Cook (ed.), *The Cinema Book*, 3rd edn (London: BFI, 2007), p. 116.

56 Rota abandoned the symphony ten years prior to reviving parts of it to score *The Leopard* (he finished it in 1972). Richard Dyer, *Nino Rota: Music, Film and Feeling* (London: BFI/Palgrave Macmillan, 2010), p. 10, says that, despite the genesis of the piece in the mid-twentieth century, '[i]f the credits did not indicate to the contrary, you might think it was a mid-nineteenth-century symphony you happen never to have heard, by Tchaikovsky perhaps.' Dyer adds that the period 'authenticity' of the symphony is consistent with both the film and the novel on which the film is based – 'all evoke an older world in something approaching the style of that world'.

57 *The Historical Novel* was first published in Russia, in a translation from the German, in 1937. The first German edition was 1955, subsequently translated into English in 1962. Geoffrey Nowell-Smith describes Visconti's reading of Lukács as 'intensive' and pairs the Hungarian thinker with Gramsci as the director's principal sources for his understanding of Marxism. See Nowell-Smith, *Luchino Visconti*, p. 215.

58 Georg Lukács, *The Historical Novel*, trans. Hannah Mitchell and Stanley Mitchell (Lincoln: University of Nebraska Press, 1983), p. 39. Further references cited parenthetically.

59 Lampedusa's novel is not divided into two parts, so what Lukács probably has in mind here are those chapters set in 1860 and 1862, i.e. during the Risorgimento, unlike the last two chapters, set in 1886 and 1910, respectively.

60 Perhaps because, in the novel, the Prince complains to Father Pirrone that he has had 'seven children' with his wife 'and never once have I seen her navel' (p. 24), Visconti adds a young daughter and a small son to the family, as well as a tutor to look after them. Those additions are not in the novel. The absence of the two children could easily have been attributable to infant mortality, given the time period of the novel, although Lampedusa does not offer any such explanation. Moreover, in the last chapter, Carolina writes a letter to 'Chiara, her married sister in Naples' (p. 265), the only reference to an additional Salina daughter. Most likely, both the 'Chiara' and the 'seven children' references result from the unfinished state of the novel at Lampedusa's death.

61 Translations from the film and the published screenplay are my own, as here, but on those frequent occasions when the dialogue from the film is identical to the novel, the lines are quoted from the Colquhoun translation of *The Leopard*, followed by a parenthetical page reference.

62 Lampedusa, *The Leopard*, p. xiii.

63 Cima, 'La realizzazione', p. 166.

64 Forgacs and Capitano, DVD commentary, *The Leopard (Il gattopardo)*, DVD.

65 'Garibaldo' instead of 'Garibaldi' might be explained as a Sicilian variant of the name based on a genealogy that has the Garibaldi family descending from one Garibaldo, Duke of Turin in 1060. See the supplement by Jessie White Mario to *Autobiography of Giuseppe Garibaldi*, 3 vols., trans. A. Werner (London: Walter Smith and Innes, 1889), p. 2.

66 Colquhoun, 'On Safari with Visconti': 11.

67 Amedeo Quondam, *Risorgimento a memoria: le poesie degli italiani* (Rome: Donzelli Editore, 2011), pp. 97–8.

68 What the Prince reads from *Angiola Maria* is elided or redacted from the original, a slightly modified version of the text over several pages; see Giulio Carcano, *Angiola Maria: storia domestica* (Milan: Manzoni, 1839), pp. 362, 364–5.

69 Once again, Visconti follows Lampedusa in these details; see *The Leopard*, p. 149.

70 Denis Mack Smith, *Victor Emanuel, Cavour, and the Risorgimento* (London: Oxford University Press, 1971), pp. 289–90.

71 Raymond Angelo Belliotti, *Values, Virtues, and Vices, Italian Style: Caesar, Dante, Machiavelli, and Garibaldi* (Teaneck, NJ: Fairleigh Dickinson University Press, 2020), p. 172.

72 See Brendan Hennessey, *Luchino Visconti and the Alchemy of Adaptation* (Albany: State University of New York Press, 2021), p. 122.

73 Andrea Merlotti, 'Oath-taking and Hand-kissing: Ceremonies of Sovereignty in a "Monarchia composita", the States of the House of Savoy from the Sixteenth to the Nineteenth Centuries', in Anna Kalinowska and Jonathan Spangler (eds), *Power and Ceremony in European History: Rituals, Practices and Representative Bodies since the Late Medieval Age* (London: Bloomsbury, 2021), p. 163.

74 Mary Ellen Snodgrass, *The Encyclopedia of World Folk Dance* (Lanham, MD: Rowman & Littlefield, 2016), p. 203.

75 See Ivo Blum, 'Archeology of the Set (I): Greuze and *The Leopard*', in *Reframing Luchino Visconti: Film and Art* (Leiden: Sidestone Press, 2017), pp. 51–68, for detailed information about Visconti's use of the painting by Greuze and paintings by other artists in *The Leopard*.

76 Vera Zamagni, *The Economic History of Italy 1860–1990* (Oxford: Oxford University Press, 1993), p. 28.

77 Luchino Visconti, 'Lampedusa: vitalità e pessimismo', in Giuliana Callegari and Nuccio Lodato (eds), *Leggere Visconti* (Pavia: Amministrazione Provinciale di Pavia, 1976), p. 92.

78 Mack Smith, *Victor Emanuel, Cavour, and the Risorgimento*, p. 292.

79 'La pagina del cinema' [Movie page], newsreel, *The Leopard* (New York: Criterion Collection, 2010), BD.

80 '"Leopard" Racks Up $370,000 in Ten Days', *Variety* 230, no. 8 (17 April 1963): 4.

81 Giovanni Grazzini, 'Il Gattopardo di Luchino Visconti non ha (troppo) tradito il romanziere', *Corriere della Sera*, 28 March 1963, p. 9.

82 Quoted by Hennessey, *Luchino Visconti and the Alchemy of Adaptation*, pp. 112–13.

83 Ugo Casiraghi, 'Il Gattopardo: un affresco senza fuori', *L'Unità*, 30 March 1963, n.p.

84 Guido Aristarco, 'Il *Gattopardo* e il telepata', *Cinema nuovo* 12, no. 162 (March–April 1963): 123, 124.

85 Monica Stirling, *A Screen of Time: A Study of Luchino Visconti* (New York: Harcourt Brace Jovanovich, 1979), p. 171.

86 Quoted by David Forgacs, 'The Prince and His Critics: The Reception of *Il Gatttopardo*', in David Messina (ed.), *Il Gattopardo at Fifty* (Ravenna: Longo Editore, 2010), pp. 41–2.

87 Juan José Gómez Gutiérrez, *The PCI Artists: Antifascists and Communism in Italian Art, 1944–1951* (Newcastle upon Tyne: Cambridge Scholars Publishing, 2015), pp. 37–8.

88 Servadio, *Luchino Visconti*, p. 179.

89 Antonello Trombadori, 'Dialogo con Visconti', in Cecchi d'Amico (ed.), *Il film 'Il gattopardo'*, p. 23.

90 Buford, *Burt Lancaster*, p. 223.

91 Other major actors were voiced by Corrado Gaipa (Lancaster), Carlo Sabatini (Delon), Lando Buzzanca (Reggiani), Franco Fabrizi (Girotti),

Isa Bellini (Bottini) and Pino Colizzi (Clémenti). See Piero Spila, *Il gattopardo* (Rome: Gremese, 2021), p. 7.

92 Buford, *Burt Lancaster*, p. 232.

93 Janet L. Meyer, *Sydney Pollack: A Critical Filmography* (Jefferson, NC: McFarland, 1998), pp. 18–19.

94 Sydney Pollack, 'A Dying Breed: The Making of *The Leopard*', interview, *The Leopard*, BD.

95 'Preparing "The Leopard" English Print', *Variety* 231, no. 1 (29 May 1963): 16.

96 Bacon, *Visconti*, p. 86.

97 Lawrence J. Quirk, 'Cites Advantages of Technirama Process', *Motion Picture Daily* 80, no. 100 (26 November 1956): 2.

98 Ibid.

99 Luchino Visconti, '*The Leopard* in London', *The Times*, 17 December 1963, p. 9.

100 'Fox Warn Visconti: Shut Up or WE Sue', *Evening Standard*, 20 December 1963, p. 17.

101 For an explanation of Technirama and other widescreen formats, see Lenny Lipton, *The Cinema in Flux: The Evolution of Motion Picture Technology from the Magic Lantern to the Digital Era* (New York: Springer, 2021), especially Chapter 62, 'CinemaScope', pp. 545–54, and Chapter 66, '65/70mm and Technirama', pp. 573–8.

102 Press release, 20th Century-Fox International Classics, n.p., *The Leopard* clipping file, Billy Rose Theatre Collection, New York Public Library at Lincoln Center.

103 Richard Roud, '*The Leopard*', *Guardian*, 5 December 1963, p. 7.

104 Ibid.

105 Bosley Crowther, 'Screen: "The Leopard" at the Plaza: Burt Lancaster Stars in Adaptation of Novel', *New York Times*, 13 August 1963, p. 25.

106 Bosley Crowther, 'Making Scenery Work', *New York Times*, 18 August 1963, Section 2, p. 1.

107 Stanley Eichelbaum, 'The "Leopard" Beautiful, but Static', *San Francisco Examiner*, 9 October 1963, p. 38.

108 Robert McMorris, '"The Leopard" Doesn't Drag', *Omaha World-Herald*, 11 October 1963, p. 55.

109 Bob Thomas, '"Haunting" Excellent Film Offering', *Johnson City Press-Chronicle*, 23 August 1963, p. 10.

110 Philip K. Scheuer, 'Hero of "Leopard" Can't Change Spots', *Los Angeles Times*, 13 August 1963, p. 59.

111 Goffredo Lombardo, interview, *The Leopard*, BD. In 1962, £1 was worth 1,750 lira. The total cost of the film in today's currency is based on the Bank of England's inflation calculator. According to *Statista*, the online data platform, the recent average of film production costs in Italy is in the region of €2.4 million, about £2.1 million. Hence the production costs of *The Leopard* in 1962 work out to roughly fourteen times the cost of the average Italian film today.

112 For an argument urging the recognition of an Italian New Wave, see Stefano Baschiera, 'New Wave Italian Style', *Italian Studies* 67, no. 3 (2012): 360–74.

113 D. A. Miller, *8½ (Otto e mezzo)* (2008; London: BFI/Bloomsbury, 2022), p. 10.

114 Geoffrey Nowell-Smith, *The History of Cinema: A Very Short Introduction* (Oxford: Oxford University Press, 2017), p. 39.

115 Curiously, both Coppola and Visconti considered Sir Lawrence Olivier for the lead in their respective films. See Carlos Clarens, 'All in the Family: The *Godfather* Saga', in Alain Silver and James Ursini (eds), *Gangster Film Reader* (Pompton Plains, NJ: Limelight Editions, 2007), p. 107.

116 Julian Sancton, 'Scorsese Restores *The Leopard* and Revives Cannes's Golden Age', *Vanity Fair*, 15 May 2010. Available at: <https://www.vanityfair.com/hollywood/2010/05/scorsese-restores-the-leopard-and-revives-canness-golden-age> (accessed 15 February 2023).

117 'Martin Scorsese's Top 10', Criterion Collection, 29 January 2014. Available at: <https://www.criterion.com/current/top-10-lists/214-martin-scorsese-s-top-10> (accessed 15 February 2023).

118 Martin Scorsese, interview, *The Age of Innocence* (New York: Criterion Collection, 2018), BD.

119 Vincent Canby, 'Grand Passion and Good Manners', *New York Times*, 17 September 1993, Section C, pp. 1, 10.

120 As Hennessey puts it in *Luchino Visconti and the Alchemy of Adaptation*, p. 111, films like those made by Merchant and Ivory 'were thought to reflect Margaret Thatcher's conservative political project that sought to profit from British history and traditions by commercializing the nation's heritage industry'.

121 André Bazin, *What Is Cinema?*, Volume 2, trans. Hugh Gray (Berkeley: University of California Press, 2005), pp. 99–100, 45.

Credits

Il gattopardo/
The Leopard
Italy
1963

Directed by
Luchino Visconti
First Assistant
Directors
Rinaldo Ricci
Albino Cocco
Second Assistant
Directors
Francesco Massaro
Brad Fuller
Produced by
Goffredo Lombardo
Screenplay and
Adaptation by
Suso Cecchi d'Amico
Pasquale Festa
Campanile
Enrico Medioli
Massimo Franciosa
Luchino Visconti
Based on the novel by
Giuseppe Tomasi di
Lampedusa
Script Supervisor
Stephan Iscovescu
Cinematographer
Giuseppe Rotunno
Camera Operators
Nino Cristiani
Enrico Cignitti
Giuseppe Maccari
Stills
G. B. Poletto
Editor
Mario Serandrei

Art Director
Mario Garbuglia
Assistant Art Director
Ferdinando Giovannoni
Set Decorators
Giorgio Pes
Laudomia Hercolani
Assistant Set
Decorator
Emilio D'Andria
Costume Design
Piero Tosi
Costume Assistants
Vera Marzot
Bice Brichetto
Costumes
SAFAS
Costumes for
Mr Lancaster
and Mr Delon
REANDA
Fabrics
Filippo Haas & Sons
Make-up
Alberto De Rossi
Hairstylists
Maria Angelini
Amalia Paoletti
Music
Nino Rota
Giuseppe Verdi
(unpublished waltz)
Music Performed by
Orchestra Sinfonica di
Santa Cecilia
Musical Director
Franco Ferrara
Sound Engineer
Mario Messina

Production Companies
Titanus
La Société Nouvelle
Pathé-Cinéma
Société Générale
Cinématographique
Executive Producer
Pietro Notarianni
Production Managers
Enzo Provenzale
Giorgio Adriani
Production Supervisors
Roberto Cocco
Riccardo Caneva
Gilberto Scarpelli
Gaetano Amata
Bruno Sassaroli
Production Secretaries
Umberto Sambuco
Lamberto Pippia
Uniforms Consultant
Alessandro Gasparinetti

uncredited
Production Company
20th Century-Fox
Make-up
Robert J. Schiffer
Hairstylist
Giancarlo De Leonardis
Special Effects
Technician
Dino Galiano
Grip
Vladimiro Salvatori
Electrician
Francesco Brescini
Camera Loader
Piero Servo

**Dialogue
(French version)**
René Barjavel
**Voice Dubbing
(Anna Maria Bottini)**
Isa Bellini
**Voice Dubbing
(Giuliano Gemma)**
Gianni Bonagura
**Voice Dubbing
(Serge Reggiani)**
Lando Buzzanca
**Voice Dubbing
(Pierre Clémenti)**
Pino Colizzi
**Voice Dubbing
(Claudia Cardinale)**
Solvejg D'Assunta
**Voice Dubbing
(Terence Hill)**
Franco Fabrizi
**Voice Dubbing
(Burt Lancaster)**
Corrado Gaipa
**Voice Dubbing
(Alain Delon)**
Carlo Sabatini
Dialogue Director
Archibald Colquhoun
**Assistant Dialogue
Directors**
Sydney Pollack
(English version)
Jacques Willemetz
(French version)
Unit Publicist
Lee Minoff
Choreographer
Alberto Testa

CAST
Burt Lancaster
Don Fabrizio, Prince of
Salina
Claudia Cardinale
Angelica Sedàra
Alain Delon
Tancredi Falconeri
Paolo Stoppa
Don Calogero Sedàra,
the mayor
Rina Morelli
Princess Maria Stella
Salina
Romolo Valli
Father Pirrone
**Terence Hill
(as Mario Girotti)**
Count Cavriaghi
Pierre Clémenti
Francesco Paolo
Lucilla Morlacchi
Concetta
Giuliano Gemma
Garibaldino general
**Evelyn Stewart
(as Ida Galli)**
Carolina
Ottavia Piccolo
Caterina
Carlo Valenzano
Paolo
Brook Fuller
little prince
Anna Maria Bottini
Mademoiselle Dombreuil
Lola Braccini
Donna Margherita
Marino Masé
tutor

**Howard Nelson Rubien
(as Howard N. Rubien)**
Don Diego
Rina De Liguoro
Princess of Presicce
Olimpia Cavalli
Mariannina
Giovanni Melisenda
Father Onofrio Rotolo
Franco Gulà
Mimì
Ivo Garrani
Colonel Pallavicino
Leslie French
Chevalley
Serge Reggiani
Don Francisco Ciccio
Tumeo
Tina Lattanzi
Marcella Rovena
Valerio Ruggeri
Anna Maria Surdo
**Giancarlo Lolli
(as Carlo Lolli)**
**Halina Zalewska
(as Alina Zalewska)**
Winni Riva
Vittorio Duse
Stelvio Rosi
Vanni Matterassi
Carlo Palmucci
Giuseppe Stagnitti
Dante Posani
Carmelo Artale
Rosolino Bua

uncredited
Pippo Agusta
Inna Alexeievna
Marie Bell

Omero Capanna
Lou Castel
Sandra Christolini
youngest daughter
Maurizio Merli
Augusto Pescarini
Paola Piscini
Mirella Radice Tomasi
Mirella
Amalia Troiani

Production Details
35mm/2.35:1
70mm/2.21:1
Colour (Technicolor)
Mono (Westrex
Recording System)

Release Details
Italian theatrical release
on 27 March 1963 by
Titanus
Running time:
185 minutes

US theatrical release
on 12 August 1963 by
20th Century-Fox
Running time:
161 minutes